CURIOUS, CONNECTED & CALM

HOW LEADERS ARE BETTER TOGETHER

STEPHANIE BOWN

First published in 2025 by Stephanie Bown

© Stephanie Bown 2025

The moral rights of the author have been asserted

A catalogue entry for this book is available from the National Library of Australia.

ISBN: 978-1-923225-65-7

Printed in Australia by Pegasus
Book production and text design by Publish Central
Cover design by Pipeline Design

The paper this book is printed on is certified as environmentally friendly.

Contents

Preface

Curious, Connected and Calm shows how high-performing teams work together better, to achieve consistently outstanding results. My aim is to demystify team dynamics and show leaders how the distinct roles and behaviours of all the individuals in a team can either help or hinder overall team performance. I want to empower leaders and aspiring leaders to build better teams, and equip them with the tools to bring talented people together in ways that ensures the whole is greater than the sum of its parts.

I am a behavioural scientist, a psychology graduate, and a high-performance leadership coach. In my practice, I work with leaders and their teams every day. I am infinitely fascinated by human behaviour, what drives it, and how to leverage it, to create the optimum conditions for thriving and succeeding at work.

This is my second book on how to achieve high performance at work.

My first book, *Purpose, Passion and Performance: How systems for leadership, culture and strategy drive the 3Ps of high-performance organisations*, was published in 2020. My goal then was to define *what* leaders and leadership teams need to work on to build high-performance organisations. It highlights the systems, processes and high-performance habits that leaders can adopt to enable long-term, sustainable success for organisations regardless of size, function and industry. *Purpose, Passion and Performance* evolved from 20 years as an organisational consultant working with leaders and leadership teams to put best practice, into practice.

In subsequent years, as I've worked with leaders and their teams to apply these practices, what I've observed is how these leadership teams interrelate. *How* they work together has an enormous impact on whether the strategies they devise are ultimately achieved. Culture takes root when leaders and leadership teams walk the talk. We take our cues from our leaders – how they behave determines whether the values of the organisation are lived. Their example sets the tone for the rest of the organisation. It is most important that positive team dynamics are role-modelled in the 'top' team, for this is where the dynamics of teamwork begin.

> **We take our cues from our leaders – how they behave determines whether the values of the organisation are lived.**

While the principles and practices in *Curious, Connected and Calm* can be applied to any team, I focus on leadership teams in this book, precisely because of the special nature of their impact on culture and performance. Leadership teams are the ultimate cross-functional unit. Organisations cannot achieve consistent high performance without a strong positive dynamic of teamwork and collaboration established in the top team.

CEOs who make it a regular habit to ask for feedback and admit mistakes make it safe for their executives to do the same. They foster an open dynamic of trust that results in shared accountability for results. Conversely, CEOs who make it a habit to 'blame and shame' their executives create environments of avoidance and mistrust. This is not an environment where teamwork can thrive – it is an environment in which every person must fend for themselves.

It's not just what leaders do, but what they say that drives culture. CEOs who espouse that culture is important, and yet spend 90% of executive meetings talking about sales, signal not that they care about people, but about profit. Conversely, CEOs who start meetings on safety, culture or customers, signal that they put people first, then profit.

If my first book was about high-performing organisations, this book is about high-performing teams. It highlights simple steps business leaders can take to dramatically improve the dynamic of their teams and increase their chances of achieving their strategies.

As with *Purpose, Passion and Performance*, my challenge with writing this book was turning complex theories on human dynamics into simple tools that busy people can digest and use in practice. I knew *Curious, Connected and Calm* was to be about the dynamics of high-performing teams, but it remained little more than a collection of ideas until I experienced two sparks of inspiration.

The first spark happened during a session with one of my mentors, Matt Church. Matt is a leadership expert and popular corporate speaker. He's also the founder of Thought Leaders Business School, an academy that trains thought leaders in getting their message out to a broader audience. Matt is known for motivating leaders and helping them get to the heart of what lights them up so they can share their message and inspire others.

If you've ever had a great coach or mentor, you'll know their power is in asking exactly the right question at exactly the right time. On a Friday in mid-December, during what was literally the last meeting of the year for both of us, Matt asked me a single, deliberate question: 'What is the primary example you are setting for your kids?'

In considering my answer to Matt's question, I discovered the first of two central ideas of this book. 'I am showing them how to be independent thinkers, to work hard, and to create the life they want. I want to show them that they are in control of their own lives.'

It was a blinding flash of the obvious. Up until that point, I hadn't really understood the intent behind the values my husband and I were instilling in our two boys. We were constantly questioning Byron and Lawson, then aged 10 and 12, about their beliefs and understanding of the world. We wanted to encourage them to share their views with us, and to form their own opinions, not to just parrot back what they had seen or heard at school or online. We wanted them to consider the information they received from multiple perspectives. They would often roll their eyes at us over the dinner table but every now and then we would be staggered by their empathy. Their awareness and capacity for insight is extraordinary, once we encourage them to dig a little deeper. In these moments, it's like discovering the truth of their personalities – who they really are beneath all the layers that we and our society gradually stack on them.

The second spark of inspiration happened a few weeks after that same Christmas when I finally recorded the audio book for *Purpose, Passion and Performance*. Encased in a soundproof studio and reading aloud from my own book, I realised I had already written the central idea for my second book – right there in the first chapter of my first book.

'*These are high-performing teams: teams that effectively leverage collective capacity to achieve team synergy, where the whole is greater than the sum of its parts.*'

It was another blinding flash of the obvious. Taken together, I had articulated the belief system that had subconsciously guided the way I work with leaders and leadership teams for decades. That is, that it's through a *combination* of high-quality independent thinking by every member of a team, with a shared intent to leverage their collective wisdom, that teams come together to achieve synergy.

Synergy is not a new concept. Human Synergistics – a global company devoted to the research and practice of team synergy (as their company name suggests) – defines it simply as being *better together*. That is, the whole team performs better together than any individual could do alone. And while this is a simple concept to define, it is notoriously difficult to achieve.

That's because we are human. In every human grouping, there exists an underlying dynamic, or natural interaction, that will either elevate members of the group to new heights or slowly, surreptitiously, unravel them. When we synergise with others, the dynamic feels good. We're in a dance, moving together in time to the music. We feel safe to show up as ourselves and challenge others in ways that elevate both thinking and enjoyment for everyone. When the dynamic is dysfunctional, we resort to defence mechanisms. We retreat – emotionally, mentally and even physically – putting up barriers to success, and even subconsciously sabotaging the performance of the group as well as ourselves.

As humans we are capable of both self-actualisation and self-destruction. My hope is that readers, when empowered with the knowledge and tools within this book, will choose more of the former and less of the latter when it comes to working with others.

Leadership teams are, by definition, made up of high-performance people. But not all leadership teams are high performing, and not all organisations are achieving sustained success. I hope that in this, my second book on performance, I can provide leaders and aspiring leaders with the tools they need to succeed as a team – by overcoming the natural barriers to collaboration and realising the full potential of their shared capabilities. And surely there's some synergy in that!

Introduction

My goal with this book is to define how leaders and leadership teams can be better, together. To provide simple, proven methods for leaders to find team synergy and avoid dysfunction.

Whether you're a company director serving on a board, an entrepreneur, an established C-suite executive, a middle manager, or an aspiring leader, the tools and techniques in this book will empower you to lead teams to achieve outstanding outcomes that serve not only the business, but the growth, learning and fulfilment of all team members.

As an organisational consultant and high-performance leadership coach, I work with CEOs, founders and executives to help them realise their visions for growth and success. Clients reach out to me because they recognise that they have a great product and great people but there is something missing in the way their people are working together. They have usually done all the right things, ticked all the right boxes, including:

- defined the company purpose and vision for growth
- hired exceptional talent
- created an organisational structure – with leaders responsible for teams
- set clear benchmarks for performance
- communicated consistently.

They have done all of this – but they still feel like they are carrying all the responsibility, accountability and risk. They are still acting like referees, managing issues between people that should have been dealt with directly. They are still being asked to weigh in on decisions they've already empowered their people to make. They are inviting input and encouraging people to speak up but being presented with lacklustre or 'safe' ideas that don't fill them with confidence that their people 'have this'. They are frustrated, stressed and somewhat disappointed, but fear that sharing their feelings with their peers and colleagues won't help and may, in fact, make things worse.

Just getting the right people in the door does not guarantee they will work well with others and unlock creative potential. The true potential for the organisation lies not solely in the brilliance of its individuals, but in the synergy and collaboration fostered within teams.

At work, while we each have individual accountabilities, it's in teams where the work gets done. Teams are the ultimate performance unit of organisations. In teams, we translate big-picture goals and strategies into daily plans and actions. In teams, we coordinate effort, trial, error, learn, revise and adapt. As Margaret Mead's famous quote suggests, often the innovations that propel organisations forward are rooted within the interactions of a few committed individuals working in teams.

Teams working in sync make magic. Google was the result of two graduate students from Stanford University, Larry Page and Sergey Brin, who were looking for better ways of extracting meaning from the mass of data accumulating on the internet. Apple Computer Inc was founded by two college dropouts, Steve Jobs and Steve Wozniak, who wanted to make computers small enough for people to have them in their home or office. The Air Jordan was the brainchild of Nike marketing executive Sonny Vacaro and creative director Peter Moore, who wanted to design a sneaker specifically for the then rookie basketballer Michael Jordan.

Teams are not just productivity and innovation hubs, they are hubs of human experience. Team life is an enormous part of work life. In teams, we forge camaraderie and experience a sense of belonging. In teams, we learn about the company culture, the ways of the business, and the skills we need to be successful. In teams we set our standards for growth, form career aspirations and take calculated risks. In teams, we celebrate wins and share losses. Our team has the potential to make or break our daily work life.

In my first book, I introduced the 3Ps of high-performing organisations: Purpose, Passion and Performance.

In this book I'd like to introduce the concept of the 3Cs of high-performing teams: Curious, Connected and Calm.

There are three qualities that, once cultivated in teams, allow them to attain and sustain a high level of performance and be better, together.

To be *better together*, leadership is required. Leadership, to my way of thinking, encompasses both self-leadership and team leadership. To lead the self is to be curious – empowering yourself to share your unique thoughts, feelings and experiences. To lead others is to be connected – to form bonds of trust and respect that encourage input and allow for different perspectives to coexist. Leading together requires calm – to unite members with firm trust and unwavering belief in your capacity as a team to respond with confidence to challenges and opportunities as they arise.

This book shows you how to lead a high-performing team. Whether you're a CEO, a team leader, or just starting out, it describes the three key qualities of high-performing teams, and how you can cultivate these to activate the potential of the people you're teaming with.

Let's look at each in detail:

- To be curious – you need to develop independent thinking.

- To be connected – you need to leverage collective capacity.

- To be calm – you need to find team synergy.

High-performing teams are teams in synergy, where independent thinkers come together and leverage collective capacity. Where skilled and talented individuals build their capacity to share, stack and combine their intelligence. Where the goal of teamwork is about thinking and learning together, to influence others and be influenced in ways that build knowledge, awareness and insight for the group.

By learning these skills, you can lead any team in any context to meet consistently high standards of performance, regardless of tenure or positional hierarchy. Leaders can be better together, by applying the principles and practices outlined in this book, to find team synergy.

Part I

Why We Need
High-performing Teams

'Never doubt that a small group of thoughtful,
committed citizens can change the world;
indeed, it's the only thing that ever has.'

Margaret Mead

1

It's not enough just to hire great people. We need great teams.

With global talent shortages putting pressure on organisations, there is strong emphasis on attracting and retaining the right talent. The value of exceptional people cannot be underestimated. However, just hiring great talent is no guarantee for great performance. Leaders who foster cultures where teamwork is emphasised encourage their people to work together in ways that enable adaptation and innovation – capabilities that are critical in the face of rapid technological advancement.

The human race certainly is racing! As we round the bend at breakneck speed into the era of artificial intelligence, leaders in every context are adapting to a host of macro-economic trends that are changing the way we live and work. Variously known as the era of AI, the fourth industrial revolution, or the era of advantaged digitisation, the current era of technology disruption is increasing the pace of change at a rate that is challenging large sub-sets of the working population to keep up.

The World Economic Forum (WEF) publishes a bi-annual *The Future of Jobs* report on the changing nature of the global workforces. In 2023 respondents from over 803 companies across all world regions reported that over a third (34%) of all business-related tasks are performed by machines. This number is set to double so that by

2030, more business-related tasks will be completed by machines than by humans.

While millions of jobs will be replaced by machines, we are in no danger of running out of work to do! The combined macrotrends of new emerging technologies, the adoption of Environmental, Social and Governance (ESG) standards, and the localisation of supply chains are predicted to deliver a net positive impact on job creation. Our challenge will not be in not having enough work for the population, the challenge will be upskilling and reskilling workers quickly enough to meet new job demands.[1]

The skills gap that is emerging is being created on two fronts. The first is the increasing demand for technology-related roles and decreasing demand for administrative and clerical roles, as mentioned in the WEF report. The second is the increasing demand for the type of work that only humans can do.

James Merisotis is the author of *Human Work* (2021) and president of the Lumina Foundation, which exists to improve pathways to learning beyond high school. Merisotis predicts that AI will ultimately lead to automation of virtually all tasks that are repetitive or can be reduced to an algorithm. Preparing for this new era of 'human work' means developing our human capacities such as compassion, critical thinking, ethics and interpersonal communication. He predicts that 'across all occupations (in 2024), half of all tasks are uniquely human, compared to just 30% of tasks in 2000. Projections of these trends suggest this number could rise to 80% in the next ten years' (p. 7).

The skills gap is real, it's widening, and it's being felt everywhere – from small regional towns to large metro cities in just about every industry, but particularly in the tech sector where, in Australia, skills shortages are listed as the #1 inhibitor of growth. We are feeling it because we are failing to skill, upskill, or reskill quickly enough.

---

1 Fastest-growing roles are technology-related roles: AI and Machine Learning Specialists, Sustainability Specialists, Business Intelligence Analysts, Information Security Analysts, Renewable Energy Engineers, Solar Energy Installation, and System Engineers. Fastest-declining roles are clerical or secretarial roles: Bank Tellers, Related Clerks, Postal Service Clerks, Cashiers, Ticket Clerks, and Data Entry Clerks. (WEF, 2023, p. 6.)

While governments and educational institutions can play their part in closing the skills gap, the onus is on businesses, and more specifically, people in business. For leaders, this means prioritising learning activities and providing workers with ample time for learning and applying new skills on-the-job. It also means embracing more flexible working options and adopting hybrid models where workers can be part of virtual teams, distributed work units or remote workforces that open access to skillsets regardless of geography.

For workers, this means taking a proactive approach to setting and achieving our own learning and development goals, asking for learning support, and being open to changing established ways of working. This is uncomfortable for many – particularly the generations who did not grow up as digital natives.

The place where this change needs to happen is in teams. We need to activate the collective pool of intelligence of our existing workforces and realise their full potential to not just meet the demands of today but prepare for the change of tomorrow. This is not just a government challenge, this is a challenge for the business sector, education institutions and communities everywhere.

> **We need to activate the collective pool of intelligence of our existing workforces and realise their full potential to not just meet the demands of today but prepare for the change of tomorrow.**

We need to treat the process of learning and performing at work as simultaneous activities, because the place where adults do most of their learning is on-the-job, in and between teams. While formal education, training and coaching (virtual or otherwise) have their place in transferring bite-sized parcels of skills and knowledge, it's through the daily interactions within our teams where learning actually sticks.

Our capacity to adapt to these changing global market forces comes down to the individuals and teams who are adopting new technologies, implementing ESG strategies, dealing with cybersecurity breaches, addressing supply chain issues, adapting to the rising cost of living and responding to changing customer expectations.

Individual and organisational success depends not just on hiring great people, but on how well those people show up and combine their talents to learn, problem solve, innovate, test and adapt. The place where each one of us can succeed in the current climate of rapidly advancing change is right at work, in our very own teams.

SMELLS LIKE *TEAM SPIRIT*

If you've worked in a team, you will have experienced how important the team dynamic is to its overall success.

The team dynamic emerges from the interplay of behaviour whenever people come together in groups to achieve a collective purpose. Each member of the group both influences and is influenced by all other members. This interplay is the sum of its parts and is, itself, the life of the group.

Social scientists working at British non-profit The Tavistock Institute in the 1960s adopted a systems approach to thinking about how humans interact within groups and organisations. They first formed the idea of the 'group-as-a-whole' or a group as having a life of its own distinct from, but related to, individual group members. Psychoanalyst Wilfred Bion, who trained at Tavistock, coined the term 'élan vital' to describe the group's 'vital force' that forms as the sum of its parts. Today, we simply call it team spirit.

While this may sound a little esoteric, it makes perfect sense when you think about it. Different teams just *feel* different – even when they exist to serve the same purpose in the same organisation or context. Anyone who has joined more than one book club in the same hometown, or worked in different teams within the same company, or played in different squads of the same club, will attest to this. Every individual is unique, and each team serves its own unique purpose. The team dynamic is the result of the unique interplay of individual personalities, their roles, and the purpose of the group.

The team dynamic is not something we often stop to observe. Like a shadow, it only appears when we cast light upon it. Through my practice partnering with hundreds of leaders and dozens of teams in

Australia and around the world, I've observed that very few voluntarily stop to look at their dynamic and assess not just what they are *doing*, but how they are *being*.

ARE YOU A TEAM OR A GROUP?

In my work as a high-performance leadership coach, I've partnered with hundreds of teams who think they are a team, but really are working as a group. Leadership teams often fall into this trap. They are called the 'leadership team', but they are thinking and behaving as a group.

This matters when it comes to working on the team dynamic, because working as a team is characteristically different to working as a group. There are different expectations that change the nature of the ways individuals work together in a team, summarised in the table below.

Working as a team	Working as a group
Interdependent	Independent
Collaboration	Cooperation
Shared goals and measures	Individual goals and measures
Shared purpose	Individual purpose

What differentiates working as a team vs working as a group? Let's consider each in turn.

1. Interdependence vs Independence

Teams work in **interdependent** ways – members have shared responsibilities and accountabilities. For example, sales teams are interdependent in achieving revenue targets. Sales and Marketing teams are interdependent in accessing or deepening market segments. Sales and Operations teams are interdependent in meeting customer expectations. Leadership teams are interdependent in fostering a culture that enables achievement of an organisation's strategy.

Groups operate in **independent** ways – members have independent responsibilities that don't rely on one another to be achieved. For example, support services such as People and Culture, Finance, Legal and Facilities Management are often grouped together and can sometimes report to the same executive but essentially operate independently from one another. Even within People and Culture teams, there can be further sub-divisions based on the size of the organisation. This can include recruiters, industrial relations specialists, learning and development specialists and payroll officers who mostly operate independently, rather than collectively.

2. Collaboration vs Cooperation

A team **collaborates** – they seek each other's involvement. A group **cooperates** – they seek each other's support. The difference between collaboration and cooperation is subtle but important. Collaboration involves building something *together* – *with* others instead of *for* others. An example is when a leadership team comes together to build a new strategic plan, the optimal outcome will be achieved if the plan emerges through the interactions of the team rather than through the efforts of one or a few individuals.

Co-operation is about bringing something to the table for which you are seeking buy-in. It may be to support a project you are implementing, or to give you feedback on a new change you're leading. An example is when a People and Culture team proposes a new parental leave policy and seek the cooperation of the business to communicate and implement it.

3. Shared goals and measures vs Individual goals and measures

Teams have **shared goals and key performance indicators**. Their performance depends on teamwork. A group has **individual goals and measures**, individual performance is rewarded.

An example of a shared goal is a revenue and profit target that applies to every executive in the leadership team, rather than separating a revenue goal for the sales executive and a margin goal for the finance executive, and so on. Making both executives accountable for not just the sales but the margin achieved, encourages them to work together to achieve it.

Similarly, setting an engagement target that applies to all leaders in the business, ensures that every people leader shares the responsibility of creating a positive experience for all employees.

4. Shared purpose vs Individual purpose

A team has **shared purpose** – a clear reason for working together. A meaningful cause that aligns the efforts of every member. Without a call to action, or a clear why for working together, individuals remain a group.

A group is a collective of people with their own **individual purposes** that may or may not align and hence there is no clear reason or benefit for working together. Groups come together for many reasons. It may be for learning (like in training and education), for sharing or communicating information (like updates and town halls), or for enjoyment reasons. This is not a reason to work together. This is a reason for being together, because it's of mutual benefit for each person, and each person is taking something beneficial away.

It is possible to be part of multiple teams at once. For example, a single individual can be a team player in:

- **A functional team:** These are teams with tangible deliverables including Sales, Marketing, Digital, Operations, Legal, People and Culture, Technology, Finance, or any of the many sub-teams that sit within those categories.

- **A leadership team:** The people who lead teams at different levels in the organisation. This could include the executive team (those who report to the CEO or 'Big Boss'), the senior team (leaders who report to the executive), or regional leadership teams (leaders responsible for a region or area).

- **A board of directors:** The governing committee of the organisation.

- **A committee:** A team appointed for a specific function.

- **A project team:** A cross-functional team who work together to deliver a specific project.

- **An office team:** A team who belong to a specific geographical location – like the Germany team, Vietnam team, or Albury Wodonga team.

This does not even cover the myriad roles that exist outside the work domain. Sport teams, volunteer teams, book clubs, community groups, and families to name a few. How many roles in how many groups do you play right now?

Most of us move seamlessly in and out of the various roles we play without a moment's thought. However, it pays to be mindful of when you are working as a team versus when you are working as a group, because this changes the nature of the role you play in each context.

Working as a team is especially important for leadership teams, who are the ultimate cross-functional team. They are called a team, but most often behave like a group – a collective of individuals who happen to report to the CEO and mostly operate independently of each other. This is the most common mistake that leadership teams make, and this poses a significant opportunity cost to business.

> Working as a team is especially important for leadership teams, who are the ultimate cross-functional team.

Now that we understand the difference between a team and a group, let's explore how the dynamic of the team directly impacts their performance.

2

From dysfunction junction to finding team synergy

The team dynamic has a big impact on team performance. Teams can either interact in healthy and high-functioning ways, or they can interact in destructive and dysfunctional ways. I call this being stuck in dysfunction junction.

The relationship between group dynamics and performance is summarised in the diagram below.

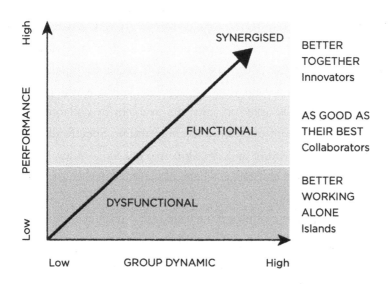

Dysfunctional teams deliver **low performance**. They are bringing out the worst in each other and are actually **better off working alone**. Members of these teams are operating like **islands**. They are often highly skilled and talented people who are more focussed on serving their own interests than the interests of the group.

Functional teams deliver an **average performance**. They are **as good as their best** – performing as well as their strongest individual. Functional teams are **collaborators** – they allow the member with the most expertise to lead and collaborate well to achieve a positive collective performance.

A **high-performing team** is a team in **synergy**. These teams are **better together** – delivering a better result together than any one individual could do alone. These teams are **innovators**, they leverage collective intelligence to identify new solutions to existing challenges.

TEAMS FIND SYNERGY ONLY A THIRD OF THE TIME

I have been helping leadership teams face the music and diagnose their dynamic for over 20 years. Human Synergistics, a global research organisation specialising in behavioural diagnostics, provides a team simulation activity that I regularly use to find out whether teams are stuck in dysfunction junction, or are finding team synergy.

In the simulation, I give a problem-solving task where they must rank a list of items according to an objective such as surviving or maximising effectiveness. They first perform a task individually working in silence, then as a team working together. When working as a team they are specifically asked to solve the problem by collaboration and consensus, over confrontation and compromise. Specifically, they are asked not to use voting as a decision-making tool – they must work together to achieve consensus where all players agree on the best solution to the problem.

Once they have completed the team task – usually within a specific time limit – they compare their solutions with the expert solution to assess their performance.

Performance is scored on based on two variables: 1) how close the team are to a solution provided by an 'expert' – someone with deep knowledge in the challenge being solved. 2) how well they leverage the collective wisdom of the group, or how close the team average score is to the 'best' individual score.

When comparing the team scores to individual scores, if the team performs *worse* than their *average individual* (individual scores averaged by the number of people in the team), they have failed in their efforts together. The group did not fully utilise the knowledge and skills available, and as a result, individuals performed better than the average of their interactive efforts. These teams are dysfunctional – they are better working alone than they are working together.

If the team performs *as well as* the *best individual* in the team – i.e., if the team score matches the best individual score – they have performed well but not achieved synergy. Members were able to tap into the knowledge and skills available in the group but were unable to convert a better result. These are functional teams – they are as good as their strongest individual.

Team synergy is achieved when the team score is *better* than the *best individual* in the team. That is, the team performed better together than any single individual could do on their own. They were able to not just tap into the knowledge and skills of every member but build on ideas to produce a stronger result. These teams are synergised – they're better together.

> **Team synergy is achieved when the team score is *better* than the *best individual* in the team.**

How often do teams find synergy? In my experience working with dozens of teams, I've observed about one in five teams find synergy in their first attempt, or about 20% of the time. Human Synergistics research suggests this occurs a little more often, but still less than half the time, on average only 36% of the time (Szumal, 2000; p. 9). That means that most teams are underutilising the collective intelligence available to them, most of the time.

I ran this exercise with a large sales team as part of their annual sales conference in Chicago. The large group of 50 or so attendees worked in smaller groups of eight to complete the exercise. In large, live forums like that, it's easy to observe why some teams find synergy while others are functional or even dysfunctional. After tallying up the scores of each table team, I asked the tables to have a frank and honest conversation about what behaviours either helped or hindered their group performance. They came up with these answers:

Dysfunctional teams (team score was worse than their average score)	Functional teams (team score was the same as their best individual score)	Synergised teams (team score was better than their best individual score)
No agreement on the goal of the task	Initial enthusiasm, 'jumping in'	Considered planning: upfront agreement on the goal of the task and how to manage time
Dominant members taking up the airspace	Realisation that planning was needed after some time was lost in debate	Delegation of roles – chair, timekeeper, note taker, etc.
Disengagement of individual members (checking phones, switching off)	'Going along with' whoever had the most perceived experience	Open invitation of all viewpoints – equally sharing the space
General low level of agreement with the team rank	Poor consideration of options	Balanced consideration of views
Poor time management – a rush to finish	Rushed approach to completion	Used the time well
An atmosphere of either conflict or boredom	At atmosphere of urgency	An atmosphere of enjoyment and humour

You'd think that the table teams who reported dysfunctional results would be more reticent to share these views – but the opposite happened! Because it was only a simulation and not the real deal, we were all able to have a good laugh about the experience and reflect on times we'd been stuck in dysfunctional teams in the past (or even in the present(!). Learning as much from our mistakes as from our successes, and not taking ourselves too seriously (while taking our work very seriously), is a big part of being able to improve via this exercise. More on this in Part IV.

If most of us are hovering in the range of functional to dysfunctional – this is actually a good news story. This means there is so much more creative potential that exists in teams already, just waiting to be activated!

Let's explore what's going on in each of these dynamics.

DYSFUNCTIONAL TEAMS

Dysfunctional teams deliver poor performance. In dysfunctional teams, individuals are **better off working alone** because they actually have a negative effect on each other's thinking. They are made up of strong individual contributors who are not team players, or at least have not been taught the skills to collaborate. They let dysfunctional dynamics get in the way, dampening their collective intelligence and reducing the efficacy of their decisions.

Remember the seven deadly sins? When it comes to teams, there are five deadly dysfunctions that if present, will drastically impact the capacity of the group to think, share, listen or make decisions. Patrick Lencioni, president of management consulting firm The Table Group and author of 2002 bestseller *The Five Dysfunctions of a Team*, developed his principles after observing and coaching thousands of CEOs and Fortune 500 management teams. For the past 20 years, his book has been *the* reference book for defining team dysfunction.

He lists the five dysfunctions as:

1. absence of trust

2. fear of conflict

3. lack of commitment

4. avoidance of accountability

5. inattention to results.

Absence of trust is represented as the foundation principle in a pyramid model, with *fear of conflict* stacked on next and so on until *inattention to results* arrives at the tip.

In this model, trust is the starting point. Trust must start with the CEO or team leader who sets the tone by their example. Without trust, we cannot feel safe to openly share dissenting views and challenge prevailing ideas. Without sharing views, we can't 'buy in', and without buying in, we can't meaningfully take accountability. Ultimately, with all this energy put into emotional manoeuvring, we lose sight of results.

Dysfunctional dynamics emerge because the individuals in the team are behaving like islands – thinking and acting in siloed ways.

Operating like an island works well in careers that are built for solo performance. Tennis players, surgeons, dentists, academics, artists, authors and solopreneurs (sole traders) all do well operating as islands. These people may have support teams but their output does not depend on team interaction – their performance is entirely within their own control.

Operating like an island is not great if you are an employee in an organisation or if you are an entrepreneur trying to scale a business. Entrepreneurs learn early the necessity of delegation and empowerment as a driver of growth. The key challenge that entrepreneurs and founders face is creating a culture of shared ownership – so that everyone 'thinks like an owner' – holistically and in the best interests of the business, and not like a 'silopreneur' in the best interests of themselves or their own departments.

Silopreneurs are people who create mini fiefdoms in organisations that lead to siloed and disconnected ways of operating. Silopreneurs believe that as long as they deliver their mandates, they are safe. They unwittingly create blockers to performance when they fail to connect their priorities to the priorities of the business.

Organisations unwittingly encourage silopreneurs when individual performance is incentivised. To foster collective action, incentives should be set up as such – so that the achievement of whole-of-business performance metrics is the first stage-gate to unlocking rewards before individual achievement is acknowledged.

FUNCTIONAL TEAMS

Functional teams are as good as their best performer. In functional teams, the team does a good job of identifying the 'best person' or the one with the most knowledge and skills for the task and letting them lead. They are good **collaborators** – they seek involvement from one another and lean into the expertise of their strongest performer to perform a task or solve a problem, as a team. Therefore, they typically perform to the level of their best individual. But they are missing a crucial but important step – building on the best ideas and turning them into something better.

Doing better means going one step further than letting the 'expert' in the team be the main decision-maker. Such as when the Marketing executive is asked to advise and decide on the best positioning for a new product category. Or when the People and Culture executive is asked to decide on how to improve the wellbeing of every member of the organisation. This is a perfectly normal practice and will produce a perfectly average result. These individuals are specialists in their fields, but their thinking can be amplified when it is tested and extended by the wisdom of the group.

Switching from dysfunctional to functional, according to Lencioni, starts with systematically building trust. The presence of trust creates a psychologically safe environment, encouraging more sharing and a diversity of viewpoints.

The more functional the team dynamic, the greater the tolerance for diversity and difference. The more open we can be to different points of view, the more rigorous we can be and ultimately this leads to better buy-in, a better quality of decision-making and ultimately better results.

More often than not, decisions that are made at the senior executive level are decisions that will affect the whole organisation. Therefore, they will benefit from being considered holistically. We experience the magic of synergy when team members invite more viewpoints and build on ideas – road-testing them and using the collective wisdom of the group to reach a point that everyone can buy into and collectively deliver on. That's what transforms functional teams into synergised teams.

SYNERGISED TEAMS

Synergised teams are better together – they are **innovators**. It is the combination of seemingly disparate ideas that come together in unique ways that enable them to invent new solutions, create new opportunities and even disrupt entire markets.

Synergised teams are high-performing teams. They are each contributing the best of their ability, and actively leveraging the collective capacity of the group. Their performance is far superior to teams stuck in dysfunction junction. Compared to dysfunctional teams, Human Synergistics research demonstrates that teams in synergy report:

- 97% more group consensus

- 96% more team effectiveness

- 69% more solution quality

- 62% more perceived synergy

- 48% more group commitment

- 60% less time wasted.

Innovation is not just a nice to have, it's a must have in today's operating context of uncertainty, technological advancement, regulatory change and economic volatility. Leaders who excel at facilitating cultures of innovation understand that individual brilliance is magnified when great people are empowered to come together to achieve great things.

Pixar Animations is an example of an organisation that excels at innovation. Throughout the 1990s they produced both technological and artistic breakthroughs in the field of computer animation that have brought us some of the most memorable and highest-grossing films of all time including the *Toy Story* series, *A Bug's Life*, *Monsters Inc.*, *Finding Nemo* and *The Incredibles*.

> **Innovation is not just a nice to have, it's a must have in today's operating context of uncertainty, technological advancement, regulatory change and economic volatility.**

Ed Catmull is the Co-Founder of Pixar and served as the CEO for just over 30 years, ultimately moving to the President of Walt Disney Animation after Disney acquired the company in 2006. Catmull started out as a computer scientist and got his big break working with George Lucas on the original Star Wars films. He is not only credited as a founding father of computer animated film, but also as a talented leader capable of building cultures where creativity and innovation thrive.

Catmull is a firm believer in the combination ideas stemming from diversity of talent as core driver of innovation. In an *HBR* article he penned, he shares his beliefs that 'creativity involves a large number of people from different disciplines working effectively together to solve a great many problems' (p.3).

Catmull goes on to write that talented people are crucial to success and indeed hard to find, but that talented people working together is an even more important and challenging prospect:

> *What's equally tough, of course, is getting talented people to work effectively with one another. That takes trust and respect, which we as managers can't mandate; they must be earned over time. What we can do is construct an environment that nurtures trusting and respectful relationships and unleashes everyone's creativity. If we get that right, the result is a vibrant community where talented people are loyal to one another and their collective work, everyone feels that they are part of something extraordinary, and their passion and accomplishments make the community a magnet for talented people coming out of schools or working at other places. (p.3).*

Pixar Animations under the leadership of Ed Catmull has created the conditions for individuals to bring their collective brilliance together and leverage shared talent.

Now that we've established that the key to being a high-performing team is finding team synergy, let's look at the special role that leadership teams play in creating cultures of high performance.

3

The tone from the top

To activate the 'team' in 'leadership team' is to sound a tone that resonates throughout the whole organisation.

Even though we often refer to C-suite, or the people at the top of the organisational tree, as the 'leadership team', the reality is they more often operate as a group – a collective of individuals, operating as 'silopreneurs', thinking and operating in siloed ways.

> **To activate the 'team' in 'leadership team' is to sound a tone that resonates throughout the whole organisation.**

Too often I come across leadership teams which don't actually work as a team. Executive 'team' meetings are often exercises in informing each other of their respective activities in their own departments. At best, these meetings are polite exercises in avoiding colliding with each other like bumper cars in a fairground ride. At worst, they're sparring contests to see who will win the debate and avoid being blamed for mistakes. When a leadership team operates in these ways, they are missing out on incredible opportunities to leverage collective capacity and generate more value for themselves, their organisation and their stakeholders.

Because of their seniority and scope of influence, how leadership teams interact and collaborate directly impacts the culture and performance of the organisations they lead. Their responsibility to act and behave like a team is magnified. They set the example for how talent can be leveraged in all teams within a business and ultimately determine the quality of the customer experience.

When the leadership team demonstrates a positive team climate of both high challenge and high trust, they make it safe for every other team in the business to do the same. That's how they influence a high-performance culture.

Leadership teams who work more like a team, define their mandate as a leadership team. This is different to the purpose of the organisation. The collective purpose of the leadership team is to foster a culture that enables the organisation to achieve its strategy. A clear leadership charter defines what their collective purpose is, where members of the team are interdependent versus independent, and where they need collaboration over cooperation. But more on this in Part IV.

The board is another version of a leadership team. Together, the board and the executive represent the power nexus of the organisation. They are the stem from which empowerment to all others flows. So, does the board need to operate more like a team? As we shall see in the next section, David Gonski AC seems to think so.

Let's explore how the board influences culture, and why the board, like the C-suite, need to work more like a team than a group.

THE BOARD IS A TEAM

In May 2023, at the Melbourne Convention Centre, business leader David Gonski AC addressed an auditorium of more than 1000 company directors as part of the Australian Institute of Company Directors (AICD) annual conference.

'A board must be a team,' he said.

Mr Gonski is somewhat of a superstar in Australian business. In his lifetime, he has served on more than 40 boards, including ANZ

Bank, ASX Limited, Morgan Stanley (Australia) and Singapore Airlines. He is currently the Chancellor of the University of New South Wales and continues to serve both executive and non-executive directorships on multiple boards. But what Mr Gonski is arguably known for most is the Gonski Report – a report he was commissioned to chair by the Australian Government regarding funding of education in Australia. The report is so famous in fact, that *'doing a Gonski'* is an acceptable Australian colloquialism when referring to schools which are implementing his recommendations.

While addressing his fellow directors at the AICD conference, Mr Gonski shared his views on what makes for a successful board career. He warned that 'group performance is something we (board members) don't spend enough time on cultivating and improving', and that 'without respect and trust, there's a danger of unpleasantness and suspicion, and that the debate, rather than assisting the company, becomes a forum for those wishing to be the standout at the meeting'.

I was keen to explore this further, so I reached out to Mr Gonski for an interview. It was an honour to speak to the living legend on the topic of board leadership, teamwork and the influence boards have on organisational culture.

In his signature style, Mr Gonski cut straight to the chase. His view is that the board must work as a team to build the level of trust and respect needed to perform to the highest level. As he told me: 'The fundamental concern I've had and worry about 'round a board table is board trust.'

For Mr Gonski, trust is fundamental to openness and therefore access to vital information that impacts company performance. 'If there is absolute trust that what's said in the room stays in the room, I think people are quite open.' Without access to the truth, boards are flying blind, and this puts not just the organisation but the directors themselves at risk.

Mr Gonski emphasises the role of the Chairperson in building trust. 'I personally think it's up to the Chairman to create that environment…. if the Chair is open and not fearing what people may say, but nurturing them, usually the reward is the table does the same.' Mr Gonski believes the Chair builds trust not by having any special rank, but by being one of the team. In other words, the Chair is 'no higher than the rest of them', but rather 'the coordinator' or 'the conductor of an orchestra if you like'.

He also stressed the importance of the relationship between the Chair and CEO in maintaining harmony and avoiding dysfunctional dynamics. 'The relationship between the CEO and the Chair is a vital one. If a board sniffs that the CEO and the Chair don't get on, they will tend to side with one or the other, and that will mean the board is fractured.'

For Mr Gonski, who serves on boards at the highest level, teamwork is almost synonymous with boardwork which involves putting egos to the side. 'If your ego can't take being in a team, then you shouldn't be on a board.' He supports the practice of boards engaging in regular self-assessment.

> **'If your ego can't take being in a team, then you shouldn't be on a board.'**

I appreciated this refreshing point of view and the emphasis Mr Gonski placed on board membership as being an act of teamwork. More importantly, I support his position that teamwork is the path to openness and truth-seeking, and that the only way this can be attained is through leadership. The Chair sets the tone and together the partnership between the Chair and CEO creates the firm foundation from which all relationship dynamics in the organisation flourish.

When asked about board impact on company culture, Mr Gonski said he believed that boards can have a great impact on culture through several mechanisms. Let's explore these in the next section.

BOARD CULTURE = COMPANY CULTURE

How can a group of men and women who meet monthly in a room and who have minimum direct interaction with an organisation except through its executive (and occasionally at site visits or social gatherings) have an impact on culture?

Apparently, quite a bit according to recent Royal Commissions in Australia into the Financial Services, Aged Care, and Disability sectors. Certainly, enough for directors to be deemed liable for corporate misconduct because of failings in company culture.

Justice Kenneth Hayne led the Royal Commission into the Banking and Financial Services sector. In his final report he found the entities, their boards and senior executives as primarily responsible for corporate misconduct, and that boards should, as often as possible, take steps to assess their organisation's culture and governance to identify and deal with problems. This includes assessing the culture of the board itself.

A similar story played out for the board of Crown Resorts, where an independent inquiry led by former Supreme Court judge Patricia Bergin, deemed Crown unfit to run a new casino at Sydney's Barangaroo, alleging that failings in leadership at the board level had ultimately facilitated money laundering and corporate misconduct.

These landmark rulings indicate that directors are ultimately accountable for culture and indeed liable for corporate misconduct, leading to legislation change.

Boards must be a team because the nature of their interactions has both a direct and indirect impact on the culture of the organisations they lead. The board, along with the executive, set the tone from the top. The board are not separate to the culture, they influence the culture by the nature of their interactions.

Boards must be a team because the nature of their interactions has both a direct and indirect impact on the culture of the organisations they lead.

While these rulings serve as fair warning for directors and boards, it also highlights a significant opportunity. If the board can work as a team, a notion supported by Mr Gonski, their collective positive impact on company culture and ultimately company performance can be significantly amplified. The board creates the climate for the CEO to feel heard, understood, and consulted in decision-making. The CEO takes that example to their leadership team. The leadership team take that example to their teams. And so on. This is how the behaviours that build teamwork, trust and collaboration spread from the core leadership group all the way through to the customer experience.

In addition, the board directly impact culture through the decisions they make about who they appoint as CEO, how they hold the CEO accountable to values and ethics of the organisation, and how they reward (or indeed punish) behaviour through incentives and remuneration.

So how can directors and executives do better? The AICD released a guidebook specifically to answer this question. Their *Governing Organisational Culture* paper suggests four ways boards can positively influence culture.

1. **Through Board processes:** Namely, through the appointment and management of a CEO whose values and principles align with that of the organisation. These are reinforced by keeping culture and strategy as regular items on the agenda and through open and honest communication between the CEO and executive team.

2. **Through Board reporting:** By paying attention to performance metrics (beyond financial ones) to review organisational performance – particularly those that indicate the health of the culture and customer experience.

3. **Through Board sensing:** By gaining first-hand experience of the culture through their participation in board committees, site visits, attendance at company events, and involvement in industry stakeholder interactions where consumers and customers attend.

4. **Through Board dynamics:** By paying attention to the culture in the boardroom and on sub-committees, i.e., how board members interact with one another and with executives. To this last point, the AICD paper asserts that: *'It is what is enacted*

around the board table – the dynamics of director decision making and discussions, their expectations and priorities, and how they hold management to account – that influences the culture that flows through the organisation.'

Board processes, reporting, and sensing mechanisms are all examples of ways boards can *indirectly* impact culture. But board dynamics – how they interact and whether they work as a team – is how board members *directly* impact culture.

It was this last point that Mr Gonski highlighted as the greatest opportunity for board improvement. He told me: 'I believe very strongly that boards have to self-assess themselves regularly, talk about how they're operating.' For him, this means going beyond the requisite board appraisal conducted by an outsider once every two to three years, to making it a regular habit after each meeting. 'I don't understand why you would have an in-camera board session before a board meeting, but I do believe in having an in-camera board session after a board meeting.' He suggests using in-camera board sessions after the meeting to check the board dynamic, as well as address the issues that in-camera sessions are usually reserved for. 'I do it relatively regularly where we actually say, 'was that meeting all right?"

Directors and leadership teams hold the greatest lever for performance. How they interact and collaborate directly impacts the culture and performance of the organisations they lead. They set the example for the whole organisation, role modelling not just *what* to do, but *how* to work together to achieve it.

While leadership teams set the tone from the top, it takes the combined efforts of all individuals working collaboratively in teams throughout the organisation to realise collective potential and drive the organisation forward. Culture is a shared responsibility – between leaders, People and Culture professionals, and every single team member. While it does not solely lie on the governing body's shoulders, they do hold the majority of the power and must recognise their influence as role models and custodians of culture.

Let's explore the three key qualities of high-performing teams and how any team, regardless of their positional authority, can cultivate these qualities by finding team synergy.

> **While leadership teams set the tone from the top, it takes the combined efforts of all individuals working collaboratively in teams throughout the organisation to realise collective potential and drive the organisation forward.**

4

Great teams are curious, connected and calm

Together is better than apart, but only if you turn up, lean in and leverage collective capacity.

High-performing teams need independent thinkers. If you've been selected to join a team, you were likely selected for your mind. When individuals hide, mask or second-guess their own beliefs and ideas, they are robbing their teams and the organisations they serve.

Similarly, high-performing teams achieve synergy by leveraging collective capacity. It's not enough just to contribute great thinking. To convert great ideas into innovative solutions, great thinking needs to be combined and leveraged. Team alchemy is achieved when the team interactions turn ideas into gold.

It's the **combination** of **independent thinking** and **collective capacity** that produces team synergy and achieves high performance. Each one alone is not enough. The diagram overleaf demonstrates how teams that are curious, connected and calm find team synergy.

Groups achieve team synergy when members contribute with rigorous independent curiosity and work collaboratively to combine creative ideas in new ways. Teams can only be effective when these two elements are present. Only under these conditions can collaboration breed innovation. By mastering these critical skills, leaders cultivate the 3Cs of high-performing teams.

Find team synergy

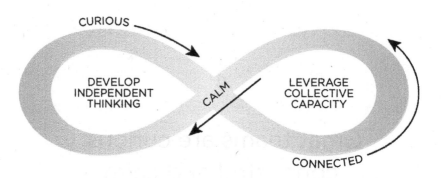

TO BE CURIOUS - DEVELOP INDEPENDENT THINKING

Firstly, great teams are *curious*. Their members are willing to think through issues, explore alternatives and share dissenting views. Curiosity opens the field of possible options available to teams by extending both the breadth (variety) and depth (quality) of experiences and ideas. When we practice curiosity, we allow more to bubble to the surface. We are more rigorous in our analysis, preventing us from falling prey to assumptions and biases that ultimately diminish the quality of our contributions.

TO BE CONNECTED - YOU NEED TO LEVERAGE COLLECTIVE CAPACITY

Great teams are *connected*. Their members are connected by clear purpose and a shared system of values and beliefs that allow them to form deep bonds of trust and immunise them against the fear of conflict. In fact, they welcome candour and dissent because they understand that through diversity of viewpoints, new ideas germinate that are ultimately better for the team and the organisation they serve. Connected teams are 'all-in'. Members are more willing to show up and be vulnerable because they value the insights that real, lived experiences can bring. They learn about one another's strengths and seek to leverage complementary strengths in the best way possible in service to their shared purpose.

TO BE CALM - FIND TEAM SYNERGY

Teams which are curious and connected will also be *calm*. They work in alignment and find team synergy. They trust in the team and hold a core belief that together, they're better. They have faith in the group process, knowing that whatever adversity comes their way, they will adapt. By maintaining calm and avoiding stress, team members maintain access to critical thinking skills at the times they need it most. They also enjoy the process of working together, seek opportunities to be together, and gain great personal value from their interactions. Great teams avoid burnout specifically because they don't create stress among one another, they create sanctuary.

These three qualities should be cultivated in yourself and the teams you lead in order to achieve sustained levels of high performance.

***

Is any of this sounding familiar? Is your team hitting it out of the park or is your team far less than the sum of their parts? Are you working as a team? Or are you a hapless group of individuals who would achieve more if you worked on your own?

I want to help you leave dysfunction junction and find team synergy, regardless of whether you are a company director, a CEO, an executive, a middle manager, an aspiring leader or an entrepreneur.

In the remaining parts of this book, and in the suggested activities contained within, you will find tools to empower you to achieve extraordinary outcomes with your people, for the benefit of your business, and to promote learning, growth and fulfilment for all.

- This book defines how leaders and leadership teams can be better together. To provide simple, proven methods for leaders to find team synergy and avoid dysfunction.

- Just hiring great talent is not enough to guarantee high performance. The true potential for the organisation is realised through the synergy and collaboration fostered within teams.

- Teams are the ultimate performance unit of organisations; the innovations that propel organisations forward are rooted within the interactions of a few committed individuals working in teams.

- Talent shortages are at an all-time high, driven by the combined macro trends of technological advancement and application of Environmental, Social and Governance (ESG) standards. Businesses with teams that prioritise knowledge transfer, upskilling and reskilling will be better enabled to adapt to these trends.

- All teams have a group dynamic that emerges from the interplay of their behaviour. This interplay is the 'sum of its parts' and is the life of the group, or the 'team spirit'.

- Working as a team means first deciding whether you are a team or a group.

  - **Teams** are interdependent. They collaborate, and have shared goals and measures, and a clear collective purpose.

  - **Groups** are independent. They cooperate, they have individual goals and measures, and they have individual purpose.

- The nature of the group dynamic has an impact on their effectiveness.

- Low-performing teams are dysfunctional – they perform worse together than their average individual. In these teams, there is an absence of trust, that leads to a fear of conflict, lack of commitment, avoidance of accountability, and ultimately inattention to results. Individuals in these teams are better working alone.

- Average performing teams are functional – the team performs as well as its strongest individual. These teams do a good job of identifying the best person for the task at hand, but fail to build on their best ideas, turning them into something even better.

- High-performing teams are synergised – the team performs better than their strongest individual. These teams adopt more constructive styles and experience greater consensus, stronger buy-in, better solution quality, and more time efficiency.

- Research demonstrates that teams find synergy only 30% of the time. This means there is so much more creative potential that exists already, just waiting to be activated!

- In dysfunctional teams, individuals behave like islands. Islands are people who are great independent thinkers but don't tap into collective capacity. This works well for people in solo careers but is detrimental to business. In organisations, these people are 'silopreneurs'; they create mini-fiefdoms that lead to siloed and disconnected ways of operating.

- Functional teams are good collaborators. They effectively identify their strongest performer and support that individual to lead the task or recommend their best solution.

- Synergised teams are innovators. They combine seemingly disparate ideas that come together in unique ways, resulting in new solutions or opportunities that have the power to disrupt entire markets.

- Even though leadership teams are called a 'team', they often behave more like a group than a team.

- Leadership teams set the tone from the top. To activate the 'team' in 'leadership team' is to sound a tone that resonates throughout the whole organisation.

- Together, the board of directors and the leadership team represent the power nexus of the organisation. They are the foundation from which empowerment to all others flows.

- The outcomes of Australian Royal Commissions into corporate misconduct have determined that company directors are not only liable for company performance, they are also liable for company culture.

- Boards influence company culture indirectly – through their appointment and dealings with the CEO, reporting mechanisms, and by 'staying in touch' with the organisation through committee memberships, site visits, social activities and customer interactions.

- Boards influence company culture directly, through the dynamic of their interactions with each other and management.

- Teams that are high performing are **curious**, **connected** and **calm**. They are able to attain and sustain a high level of performance without burning out. They are:
  - **Curious** – their members are willing to think through issues, explore alternatives, and share dissenting views.
  - **Connected** – they form deep bonds of trust that enable them to be vulnerable, share their experiences, and build on one another's ideas.
  - **Calm** – they hold a fundamental belief that together, we're better. They believe in each other's capabilities to adapt and respond regardless of the circumstances.

- Teams in synergy develop independent thinking and leverage collective capacity. Only when these two elements are present can collaboration breed innovation.

- Any team can learn to be a high-performing team. High-performing teams are:
  - **Curious** – they develop independent thinking
  - **Connected** – they leverage collective capacity
  - **Calm** – they find team synergy.

Part II

Be Curious

'I have no special talent.
I am only passionately curious.'

Albert Einstein

5

Thinking is a premium

My coaching client (let's call her Alice) is soon to be turning 60 and has reached a professional cross-roads. For 30 years, she has built her business from very humble beginnings to a highly respectable medium-sized enterprise. She has recently been offered an acquisition deal by a larger, similarly respectable, but culturally different organisation. While she is encouraged by the financial security this opportunity offers her and her family, she is also feeling conflicted.

A recent conversation with Alice went like this:

'I'm not sure I could work for anyone after being in charge for so long, and I'm not ready to retire,' Alice told me. 'What would I do? I like my work and the team I've built. If I take the offer and leave, I can't continue doing what I do now because of a non-compete clause. I'd have to think of some other way to do what I love.'

'So, then, why not turn it down?' I asked. 'Why not carry on for another 10 years and wait for the next offer to come along?'

'Because I'm afraid that if I wait too long, I'll be made redundant by AI!' Alice retorted.

We both had a laugh, but in that moment, Alice touched on an existential crisis being experienced by millions of workers worldwide. Two generations, the Boomers and Gen X, are less likely to trust smart technologies than younger generations, according to a MITRE-Harris Poll in 2023.[1] The advent of AI – or the automation of thinking – is a major disruption to the way humans work and live, as smart technology takes over more tasks that people used to do.

Consequently, for workers to stay relevant, the World Economic Forum (WEF) *Future of Jobs 2023* report anticipates that about 40% of core skills will change, and about half of all employees will need reskilling by 2025.

The WEF publishes a top 10 list of skills relevant today and in the future each year. In 2023, the top five skills that will be in demand in 2025 are:

- creative thinking

- analytical thinking

- resilience, flexibility and agility

- motivation and self-awareness

- curiosity and lifelong learning.

Why these skills? Because they are uniquely human.

Jamie Merisotis, president of Lumina Foundation and author of *Human Work* (2021), argues that to prepare for this new era, we need to work alongside smart machines and develop skillsets in the kind of work that only humans can do. These include skillsets that echo those reported by the WEF including critical thinking and reasoning, inter-personal skills, and empathy.

The nature of the game is changing, and with this comes a need for us to evolve in the very ways that elevate our humanity. Merisotis warns:

People cannot and should not compete with machines for work. We can't prepare people for human work by trying to make them more

---

1   The MITRE-Harris poll included 2063 US residents over 18 years, surveyed from July 13–17, 2023. The survey found that most Gen Z (54%) and millennials (58%) were willing to use AI to perform everyday tasks, but a much lower percentage of Gen X (39%) and boomers (30%) were willing to do so. In the same poll, 52% of employed respondents were worried AI would replace their jobs.

like machines.... Instead, people need to focus on what makes us different from machines by developing our knowledge, skills and abilities through a learning system that puts human capabilities and values first. (p.xii.)

At the root of the existential crisis expressed by my coaching client Alice and felt by many, is a fear of becoming obsolete. But as we shall see, this is not what we should be afraid of, when in fact we are more at risk of the joint epidemic's triple threat of algorithms, attention theft and burnout.

THE JOINT EPIDEMICS OF ALGORITHMS, ATTENTION THEFT AND BURNOUT

Thinking is a premium, and yet it is also the very thing that is most at risk.

We all know that when it comes to data, rubbish in = rubbish out. The same goes for our mind. What we feed it and how we use it determines the quality of our contribution and the value we add.

Modern-day workers are facing a triple threat from the joint epidemics of algorithms, attention theft and burnout.

Algorithms reinforce biases

More and more, our capacity to think, create and problem solve is being challenged by algorithms delivered through social media. Our viewpoints are being regurgitated back to us via algorithms which sense what we like, what we tolerate and what we think we need. Social media serves to reinforce existing beliefs, not challenge them. We are slowly losing the capacity for critical thinking, and this is the very capacity we need to develop as a society if we are to remain relevant and adaptive in a world where cognitive load is being managed more and more by computers.

> **More and more, our capacity to think, create and problem solve is being challenged by algorithms delivered through social media.**

Attention theft robs us of time

Attention theft is catastrophic to independent thinking and crippling our ability to focus. How many notifications are pinging right now to pull your attention away from reading these pages? How many times a day are you pulled away from the task at hand?

Research from Tania Barney, neuroscience and sensory processing expert, suggests that distractions are costing us time as well as money[1].

Her research found:

- An average of 2.1 hours are lost daily as a result of distractions.

- The average time spent on a task before we get distracted is 11 minutes.

- The amount of time it takes to return to a task after a disruption is 25 minutes.[2]

After meetings, emails, unplanned interactions and rest breaks, how many hours do we have left in a day for thinking and productive work? We get pulled into the urgent, not important quadrant of Coveys' time management matrix and this leads to the next major threat to thinking – burnout.

Burnout robs us of energy

Burnout is the compound interest on lost productivity due to attention theft. While getting distracted on the urgent, not important stuff, the important stuff does not go away. It piles up, weighing us down psychologically and eating into recreation hours where we should be recharging our batteries through rest, exercise, or time with loved ones. Burnout is a global issue, costing humans their wellbeing and businesses millions in lost productivity.

The University of Melbourne's 2023 *State of the Future of Work* report[3] reported that a startling 81% of the Australian workforce is struggling with stress and burnout, ahead of the global average of 73%.

---

1   https://www.visualistan.com/2016/06/how-to-focus-at-work-in-the-age-of-distractions.html
2   https://workplaceevents.co/how-much-time-do-you-lose-to-distractions/
3   This comprehensive study included 24,235 employees across 16 countries.

Burnout is the result of prolonged work stress. Symptoms include overwhelm, constant exhaustion and a feeling of being ineffective at work no matter how hard you try.

The World Health Organization (WHO) took the significant step in 2019 of legitimising burnout by adding it to its International Classification of Diseases.

Increased rates of burnout is bad news for business, and has been identified as one of the leading causes driving people to leave their jobs. But it also leads to disengagement, which can cost employers 34% of a disengaged employees annual salary, according to the Gallup State of the Global Workplace 2021 report.

With the joint epidemics of algorithms, attention theft and burnout, our most precious resources have changed from *time* and *money* to *energy* and *attention*.

> **With the joint epidemics of algorithms, attention theft and burnout, our most precious resources have changed from *time* and *money* to *energy* and *attention*.**

As we shall see in the next chapter, the antidote to the triple threat of algorithms, attention theft and burnout is our very human capacity for curiosity.

6

Curiosity did not kill the cat

Curiosity is an essential quality of high-performing teams because it is the antidote to the joint epidemics of algorithms, attention theft and burnout. But curiosity hasn't always had the best wrap.

Have you ever been admonished with that old phrase 'curiosity killed the cat' anytime you were poking around where you possibly shouldn't have been?

That phrase has a lot to answer for. How many generations of children have been mollified into not asking questions? Warned against seeking answers to puzzling predicaments? Shamed into tolerating the seemingly inexplicable?

How many of those children grew into adults who on a deep subconscious level believed it was impolite to dig deeper, challenge authority, speak their voice, or stand up for what is right? How many times has that idea prevented workers from asking the so-called 'stupid questions' for fear of looking, well, somewhat stupid?

That phrase needs to be cancelled, along with 'be a good girl/boy', 'don't answer back' and 'children should be seen and not heard'.

Curiosity did not kill the cat – it made the cat do very funny things that are endlessly entertaining and provide countless hours of quality scrolling to millions around the world regardless of ethnicity, language, age or status!

In all seriousness, curiosity is an essential quality in high-performing teams and organisations because it helps individuals be more resilient, makes them better learners, and is an absolute necessity to the creativeprocess.

CURIOSITY MAKES US MORE RESILIENT

To be high performing, you need to be curious about not only *how* we think and feel, but *why* we think and feel the way we do. Todd Kashdan, author of *Curious?* (2009) and lead researcher in the field of positive psychology, has demonstrated that curiosity helps us manage anxiety. It is a source of resilience when exposed to negative life events and stress.

Kashdan says that the single most powerful way to increase human happiness is to increase our capacity to tolerate, recognise and identify emotional pain. At first, this idea seems antithetical, but it has its roots in Buddhist teachings where the key to finding peace of mind is to tolerate suffering and to detach oneself from one's needs and desires.

Instead of seeing negative emotions as, well, negative, his research shows that if we can take a moment to be curious about and name the emotions we are experiencing in moments of stress, we can take advantage of the information they are trying to convey. In his keynote at the *Happiness and Its Causes* conference in 2013, he said: 'If you have a preponderance of negative emotions but you're good at being aware of them, understanding them and clarifying them, they're no longer toxic, they're just information that you can use, just as you use Google.'[1]

His research reveals that developing a healthy degree of self-curiosity (curiosity about how we think and feel) can help us withstand the potentially negative effects of stress and even enable us to appreciate the value of negative emotions like loss, pain, guilt, shame or embarrassment. These negative emotions are often precursors to action. For example – guilt leads us to make amends or overcome conflict;

---

1   https://www.youtube.com/watch?v=_7WMKmGdMIY

embarrassment leads us to better preparation or awareness of others' needs; anger ignites us with courage and motivation to right a wrong.

Emotions are data

The ultimate moment to practice self-curiosity is when we cry. How comfortable are you when someone at work starts welling up? Many of us associate shame with crying or showing any strong emotions at work. But crying is not shameful – it just shows us how much we care. I learned a useful way to hold space for people in that moment from the wonderful Sue Langley of Langley Group while completing my Diploma of Positive Psychology. There were lots of tears in Sue's class (surprisingly given it was a program about happiness!). Whenever a student started welling up and finding it difficult to speak, Sue would pause and say: 'It's OK, emotions are data!'

We do not need to ignore, control or be afraid of emotions. Emotions are rich sources of data, elegantly transmitted through nature and nurture, that keep us connected, safe, productive, and infinitely creative.

> **Emotions are rich sources of data, elegantly transmitted through nature and nurture, that keep us connected, safe, productive, and infinitely creative.**

Thriving in any environment – whether it be one of abundance or scarcity – means effectively working with and leveraging our emotions. Emotional Intelligence (EI) is a well-researched and validated capability that plays a potentially bigger part in leadership and career success than intelligence alone. The very definition of emotional intelligence is the intelligent use of emotional data in decision-making and behaviour.

When something is not right, our brains will alert us. In those moments we shouldn't disregard or stifle feelings of unease and anxiety. Instead, we need to lean into them. Be curious about them – identify them, name them, and locate the meaning behind them. Curiosity allows us to detach from the emotion *just enough* to acknowledge what we are feeling and give ourselves the chance to manage *it* before it manages *us*.

To be curious about the content of our emotions and what they are telling us is to give ourselves the psychological space necessary to make a decision about our next action.

Vicktor Frankl, Holocaust survivor and psychiatrist, said this best in his 1959 book *Man's Search for Meaning*: 'Between the stimulus and the response there is a space. In that space is our power to choose a response. In our response, lies our growth and our freedom.'

Self-curiosity is a simple and useful vehicle for strengthening emotional intelligence. To be self-curious is to explore your emotions, appreciate them for their wisdom, give them names, identify where they came from, and acknowledge them in how you choose to respond next. In these ways they provide a rich pool of experiences on which to lean during the moments where we are stretched far outside our comfort zones.

CURIOSITY MAKES BETTER LEARNERS

Curiosity is a key quality of high-performing teams and one of the top five skills of the future, because it is the antidote to fear and the key to learning. By staying curious, we remain open to thinking, to new ideas, to ways of understanding our reality without the shame of not having immediate answers. Curiosity feeds learning because it puts us into a state of inquiry – and allows us to tolerate ambiguity for the time it takes to find the joy of discovery.

On the surface, learning sounds like an enjoyable exercise. But the reality for many is that learning is uncomfortable. Learning involves challenging and questioning assumptions, beliefs, values and accepted norms. 'To learn, and thereby to change, is like a mini-death to a known way of being' (Bain, 1998, p. 416). However, in order for new learning to be gained, something old must be lost. Inherent in the process of learning, is the concurrent process of letting go.

The challenge to learning, however, is that the space of 'not knowing' is uncomfortable at best, and at worst, completely avoided. This is particularly challenging for leaders. To willingly move into a space of 'not knowing' seems antithetical to what is commonly expected of leaders and managers in modern organisations, who need to be 'in the know' at all times. To learn is to be comfortable with being uncomfortable.

Learning is only uncomfortable until we experience the joy of discovery. Finding out something new, feeling like ideas and puzzles are clicking into place, finding new ways to put into words what you only intuited – this is the joy of discovery.

To be 'passionately curious' in the words of the great Einstein, is to be uniquely human. Curiosity sparks questions. Questions spark thinking. Thinking sparks connections. Connections spark creativity. Creativity sparks innovation.

> **To be 'passionately curious' in the words of the great Einstein, is to be uniquely human. Curiosity sparks questions. Questions spark thinking. Thinking sparks connections. Connections spark creativity. Creativity sparks innovation.**

Learning is essential to adaptation – both from an evolutionary perspective and from an organisational perspective. The advent of AI and integration of smart machines is just another innovation in a long line[1] of disruptive technologies that have changed the way humans live and work. Like the invention of the printing press, the light bulb, the Model T car, the word processor, cell phones and the internet, each innovation represents a giant leap forward in augmenting human capability and allowing us to progress faster as a race.

By being curious, we remain adaptive and resilient. Curiosity is both a mindset and a skillset. It's an attitude that we can bring to the daily vicissitudes of life, and an actual skill that we can apply to solving problems. As we will discover in the next section, curiosity activates a host of benefits that not only support our mental health and wellbeing but adds incredible value to businesses and teams.

---

1   For an interesting visual graph on tech disruptions since 1000 CE, check out https://www.trustnet.com/news/13396044/two-charts-demonstrating-1000-years-of-tech-disruption

CURIOSITY MAKES US MORE CREATIVE

In his 2021 book *Think Again*, organisational psychologist and *New York Times* bestseller Adam Grant challenged his readers to think beyond their first response. He challenged us to identify that sometimes our first instinct is not the best idea. That in fact, we would benefit from thinking more like scientists – forming hypotheses and testing these out for factual accuracy rather than falling prey to ignorance, assumptions and biases.

Our lens on the world – how we see it – is coloured by our values and beliefs. These are instilled in us from birth and determine what we judge as good, bad or indifferent. Viewpoints, values and beliefs are inherited and passed down through the psycho-social cultural paradigms we're raised in. Sometimes our first instinct is not the best option because our viewpoint is limited to these viewpoints and experiences. Where did you inherit your world view? What is your familial and cultural history? How has that influenced your mindset – the things you are more fixed about versus more open about?

To be more curious is to examine our views – to test them, roll them around a bit. A sign of an evolved society is one that can tolerate different views, where free speech is a cornerstone. Most of us aspire to live in a world where people of different races, religions, sexual orientations and abilities can not only tolerate each other, but actively work together. Not only does this lead to richer cultural experiences, but it also drives innovation.

Curiosity not only opens our minds to different points of view, it sparks the creative process that leads to innovation. The key to leveraging the shared capabilities in teams begins with mining different viewpoints so that we can open the world of possibilities for consideration. To be curious about what others are thinking – why they may or may not agree with your point of view – is to invite in an essential ingredient to the creative process. That is, to open up a world of possibilities.

Curiosity not only opens our minds to different points of view, it sparks the creative process that leads to innovation.

Thinking like a scientist is about forming hypotheses that we can test and measure. Ultimately, decision-making is better because it's based on a wider view than one single, dominant perspective.

So now that we've established how critical the mindset and skillset of curiosity is to wellbeing, intellect and the creative process, how can we develop it in individuals and teams at work? To be curious, we need to develop independent thinking by first paying attention to our thoughts and doing our due diligence on them.

7

Where do thoughts come from?

As a young consultant at Nous Group – an Australian-based management consulting group – I received a piece of feedback that has stayed with me for life and challenged me to share my voice, no matter what the context.

I was accompanying a principal to a client meeting and was asked to take notes. So, that was what I did. Straight after the meeting, my colleague asked me why I was so quiet and whether I had any unanswered questions. I conceded that I was just trying to capture everything, and that, yes, I did have questions, but I didn't want to interrupt the flow, and besides, I knew I could ask her about it afterwards. She turned to me and said: 'Steph, we hired you for your mind. Use it.'

Her point was clear – at Nous there would be no hiding. We were literally minds for hire, our questions mattered. My performance depended on my ability to think critically, to step up and ask questions that opened possibilities and invited alternative points of view.

So – let's put you to the test!

On a scale of 0–2, where '0' is 'essentially unlike you'; '1' is 'like you quite often', and '2' is 'like you most of the time'; how would you rate yourself on these two statements:

I am unique and independent in thought.
I am a creative and original thinker.

On the Human Synergistics Life-Style Inventory, these two questions provide insight into the value you place on your own thinking. These items also happen to be from the 'Self-Actualisation' scale – the degree to which you feel engaged and satisfied at work. If high performance is the desired outcome, self-actualisation is the necessary input. High performance relies on people actively bringing their full selves to work – actualising their strengths and capabilities in service to what they value as a meaningful cause.

I've conducted hundreds of LSI debriefs with leaders all around the world and – like I was challenged in my Nous days – often challenge anyone who rates themselves anything less than 2 on this scale.

Typical reasons people give for rating themselves less than a 2 are:

- I don't think I'm particularly creative or unique.
- I don't have time to think or be creative.
- I'm not asked for my ideas.

To this I say – begone with your self-limiting beliefs!

Of *course* you are unique and independent in thought! As we explored in the previous section, your lens on the world is unique to you by virtue of your unique combination of values, attributes and experiences. Unless you can appreciate how your lens on the world adds value to the team or organisation you serve, how can you fully realise your potential? Unless you place a value on your ideas, how can you contribute meaningfully or lead in any context?

To be curious, we need to develop independent thinking. High-performing teams need independent thinkers. Not co-dependent repeaters.

Placing a high value on independent thinking is important for workers everywhere, especially as AI takes over cognitive processing tasks that can be automated. This will put greater demand on new and existing roles that require collaboration and creative thinking to solve. Knowing, listening to, and understanding how your voice adds value to the creative problem-solving process, as well as having the emotional intelligence to know *when* to share your voice, will be important to leaders and decision-makers in every context.

Independent thinking is especially important for key decision-makers – executives, founders, directors and investors. Their decisions impact the lives of many – their customers, colleagues, suppliers and communities. Their capacity to think creatively and critically, as well as contribute that thinking in clear and constructive ways, directly impacts business performance and value creation for all stakeholders.

> **To be curious, we need to develop independent thinking.**
> **High-performing teams need independent thinkers.**
> **Not co-dependent repeaters.**

THOUGHTS DON'T COME TO YOU, THEY COME THROUGH YOU

If we are to improve how we think, it's helpful to first understand where thoughts come from.

Have you ever stopped to wonder where your thoughts come from?

Are your thoughts your own? Are you the first person to think them? Or are you channelling them from some other source? The answer is: yes, yes and yes.

Dr Michael Muthukrishna, Associate Professor of Economic Psychology at the London School of Economics, thinks that we're both downloading from, and uploading to, a human 'cloud' of inherited knowledge. In his ambitiously titled 2023 book, *A Theory of Everyone*, he attempts to answer some rather big questions – like why humans are so different to other animals, what underlies social and cultural change, and why some societies are more corrupt than others.

In a 2024 interview with motivational speaker and leadership guru Simon Sinek, Dr Muthukrishna explained that the reason humans are different to animals is because we have evolved to transmit not just genes (hardware) but knowledge (software) through generations.

'Humans are so different to animals because we moved from just a reliance on hardware, to a reliance on hardware *and* software,' Dr Muthukrishna explained. 'Ideas and concepts have been culturally evolving and transmitted from generation to generation. Our culture has more intelligence than any of us. We are like nodes in a collective brain.'[1]

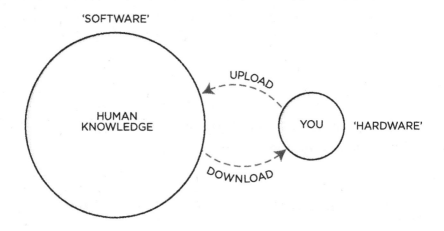

Thoughts don't come *to* you, they come *through* you.

In her 2015 book *Big Magic*, Elizabeth Gilbert (author of *Eat Pray Love*) thinks thoughts worth thinking are like butterflies looking for a place to land. They might land on you for a while, but if you don't grab them, they'll fly away and look for someone else to land on.

Thoughts don't come *to* you, they come *through* you.

Have you ever had a great idea but let it pass you buy – only to discover later that someone else picked it up and ran with it? Every time I'm in an airport travelling with my husband, he looks at the stanchions used to create queues and says: 'I thought of that when I was a kid,

---

1   https://simonsinek.com/podcast/episodes/a-theory-of-everyone-with-dr-michael-muthukrishna/

putting seatbelts in these things. I should have trademarked it!' Yep – he should have!

When I was in my early 20s, I thought one day about a reality TV competition where professional dancers had to compete by winning at every style of dance – not just their own. A year later, *So You Think You Can Dance* came on air. Should have trademarked that one also!

Some people believe there are no more truly original ideas in this world. That everything we see and read is a version of something that has come before.

So how then can you still be 'unique and independent in thought'?

Because when thoughts and ideas come *through* you, you are filtering them through your unique values, experiences and attitudes. The result is an idea or concept changed in some way. What you contribute with independent thinking is an upgrade or add-on to something that was already known. In our own small way, every time we speak or share our thoughts and ideas, we each individually add to the body of human knowledge.

Think about it like this: if I asked a class of 20 art students to paint a still-life of bananas, no single finished piece would end up the same. I would have 20 different versions of bananas, but they would all still be bananas. The same goes with thoughts.

Isaac Newton said: 'If I have seen further than others, it's because I have stood on the shoulders of giants.' We are all standing on the shoulders of giants – those who came before us, or those around us who inspire us still today.

Who are you to think your perspective is not unique? That you are not creative? When you do not think independently and contribute your perspective, you are robbing the world of the opportunity to colour an idea in a slightly different shade, see a chink in it, put context around it, or help more people appreciate it.

How could Anne Frank have ever known that her diary would inspire millions of people around the world, many decades after she wrote it? How could Napoleon and Josephine ever have imagined that their love letters would become priceless artifacts of history?

Who are you to think your perspective is not unique?
That you are not creative?

You do not know where your thoughts and contributions will go. All you can know is that by thinking and sharing your thoughts, by building on what others know, you are showing up in ways that have the potential to add value to others' lives.

WHO PUT THAT THOUGHT IN MY BRAIN?

Sometimes thoughts or ideas don't just randomly collide with us. Sometimes other people put them there.

Projection is an unconscious psychological process that works like a laser beam – where we transmit our own thoughts and feelings into others' heads in ways that make them perceive them as their own.

Projection happens when we are feeling something uncomfortable or anxiety-provoking, and we can't contain these emotions. Our emotional cup overflows, and not in a good way. So, to rid ourselves of these uncomfortable feelings, we siphon it off (project it) and send it to someone else who takes it on and feels it on our behalf (introjection). While this sounds a bit voodoo, it's more common than you think.

Have you ever been in a situation where you feel annoyed or angry because you were belittled about something at work, and then took that home and made a partner/friend/loved-one feel belittled about something entirely unrelated? Ringing any bells?!

In an effort towards self-preservation, we unconsciously send uncomfortable feelings of insignificance or vulnerability to someone else who we perceive as 'safe' to hold it for a while until we can do something with it. They are perceived as safe because they are either less powerful than us (for example, sub-ordinates at work) and therefore less likely to create consequences. Or because they are invested in the relationship with us (like friends and family) and are therefore likely to forgive us at some stage.

If, after you've calmed down and reflected on what you've done, you realise you need to apologise for your poor choice of behaviour, then you are ready to 'take it back' (re-introject). This allows you to deal with it in more constructive ways, such as having a direct conversation with the person who made you feel that way in the first place. This is when you take accountability for the transgression. Being accountable is counting the debt back into your own emotional bank account to pay it to its rightful owner – the jerk at work who needs the feedback in order to grow!

Gaslighting is projecting your nasties consistently, over time, hitting the same target over and over until they start to question their own perception of reality. Gaslighting comes from people with an inescapable need for power and control because they were made to feel powerless as children. To understand how that works – watch or read *Girl on the Train*. Not to take notes! But to understand how we can unwittingly take on other people's sh!t when we really don't have to.

Projection can also work in a positive way – this is called the **Pygmalion effect**. Pygmalion is one of the rare Greek myths that doesn't end in tragedy. As the story goes, Pygmalion was a sculptor who crafted a woman so perfect that he fell in love with her. He made an offering to Aphrodite, the Goddess of love, where he wished for a bride who would be the 'living likeness of my ivory girl'. He returned home to discover that Aphrodite had granted his wish and turned his creation into a living woman. Aphrodite must have been feeling unusually generous that day!

The Pygmalion effect was a term coined by Robert Rosenthal and Lenore Jacobson in 1969. The pair observed that teachers' high expectations of students led to improved performance, while low expectations led to worse performance. Both effects created a **self-fulfilling prophecy**.[1] This finding has since been replicated in multiple settings including in work and military settings (Eden & Shani, 1982), and medical settings (Learman et al., 1990; Jenner, 1990).

In the Pygmalion effect, people will either rise or fall to the level of others' expectations.

---

1   Self-fulfilling prophecy: a prediction that comes true at least in part because of a person's belief or expectation in themselves.

As potential senders of these projections, the message is simple – expect the best, get the best. Expect the worst, get the worst. This is particularly important for leaders, teachers and parents. Seek out potential, find strengths and believe in others' capacity for growth. They might just rise to the challenge!

Pygmalion effect

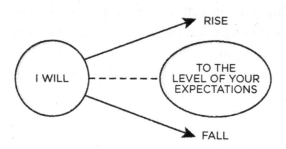

As receivers of potentially supportive or destructive psychological messages, how can we decipher whether our thoughts and feelings are our own or whether they are coming from some external source? In the end, we may never disentangle this question.

Being curious about what you think, why you think it, and whether your train of thought is helping or hindering you is a good place to start. As mentioned in Chapter 6 – being curious gives us the psychological space to name the emotion we are feeling and understand what it is trying to tell us. If we can step back from the emotion, this is often enough to be able to observe that in this situation 'it's not about me, it's about them' and to make a choice about how to respond rather than fall prey to a game that someone else may be playing.

To develop independent thinking, we need to be aware of the traps to avoid. These are called 'thinking diminishers'. We also need to learn the ways we can strengthen curiosity and critical thinking skills – or, 'thinking amplifiers'. Let's explore each of these in the following sections.

8

Ban the BANS – biases, assumptions, norms and self-limiting beliefs

When it comes to thinking, too often we get in our own way. We let fear, dogma, habit or sheer laziness determine our response.

The BANS are the cognitive shortcuts that our brains take to minimise processing effort. These are **B**iases, **A**ssumptions, **N**orms and **S**elf-limiting beliefs.

Being more aware of them is the first step towards stopping them from holding you back and making more reasoned, more creative, and better articulated decisions.

In the following pages, I'll describe the BANS and how they negatively impact the quality of our thinking and our ability to work together in teams.

BIASES

A **bias** is a tendency, inclination or prejudice toward or against something or someone.

There are two classes of bias – stereotyping and cognitive bias.

Stereotyping is a learned bias and often leads to discrimination against an individual or group based on physical characteristics like gender, ethnicity, sexual orientation, age or ability. Stereotyping can cause us to discredit or pay less attention to the insights and contributions of the 'minority' group in the room – not giving voice to the single female at the board table or ignoring the suggestions of the man of colour in an all-white leadership team. Stereotyping can also impact recruitment or promotion decisions – leading to less diversity of people and, therefore, less diversity of ideas, available to draw from in teams.

Cognitive biases are not learned. They are cognitive shortcuts that all humans are susceptible to regardless of race or upbringing. There are 20 known cognitive biases, and they all impact our ability to be curious and think independently. I've listed here some of the most insidious to teamwork and performance at work.

- **Confirmation bias** is favouring information that supports our current beliefs, while ignoring facts that go against those beliefs, despite their relevance. This is the bias that algorithms and social media play to the most. This is also the bias that political and marketing campaigns depend on. This bias can hamper team performance when individuals only present evidence to support their claims while ignoring the evidence against it. For example, presenting the business case for hybrid working while ignoring the evidence against it, or for subsets of the labour market for whom it is not preferable.

- **Conformity bias** is similar to groupthink, which occurs when we change our opinions or beliefs to match the bigger group, even if we don't necessarily agree. This is often the result of peer pressure or wanting to fit into a certain social group. When we are conforming, we are making decisions based on compromise instead of consensus. An example is: deciding to hire the candidate who the boss likes more and argues for, over the candidate with the stronger CV.

- **Authority bias** is the tendency to attribute greater efficacy to the opinion of the authority figure and be more influenced by that opinion. While the person in the highest paid position may in fact also hold deep knowledge and experience, they are not necessarily more or less valid in their view than any other member of a team of experts. In fact, a professional CEO is strong in business, but will hire subject matter experts in his or her team – in sales, marketing, production etc. – because they recognise that high-performing teams are ones with complementary skillsets. However, because of their authority as the final decision-maker, their opinion on matters of sales or marketing may hold more weight in the team and ultimately shut down contribution.

- **The illusory truth effect** is the increasing effect of information the more times we encounter it, regardless of whether it is true or false. Algorithms also play to this bias. In teams we can fall prey to it when individuals keep pushing their viewpoint repeatedly – knowing that repetition of the same message will create an impression of truth. An example is a sales leader pushing for a new product category repeatedly at every meeting, without providing the necessary market data to back up the claim. Eventually, his colleagues hear it enough times to believe it to be true.

- **The false consensus effect** is the tendency to overestimate how much other people agree with our own beliefs, behaviours, values and attitudes. This bias can make us lazy about building strong cases to support our ideas. It can also get in the way of communication – assuming more people agree and understand our directives more than is the reality. An example is a CEO sharing his or her new vision and expecting everyone to buy into it from the very start.

ASSUMPTIONS

Assumptions are things you accept to be true without question or proof.

Early in my career I led a small team at a registered training organisation (RTO). I had a great boss and she used to challenge me daily on my assumptions. She used to quote Oscar Wilde when she'd say 'When you assume, you make an ass out of u and me'.

She was right to do so – I was only 23 and she had entrusted me with managing the team while she focussed on business growth. She was checking whether, given my limited work experience, I was basing my suggestions and decisions on sound reasoning instead of basic assumptions.

> **'When you assume, you make an ass out of u and me.'**
> **Oscar Wilde**

During the global COVID pandemic, many of our assumptions were challenged. Assumptions like:

- People can't be productive when working from home.
- Children must go to school to learn.
- Hospitals are safe places.

We make assumptions based on precedents. But if the context or situation changes dramatically, as it did for everyone simultaneously during COVID, the precedents no longer hold up.

Assumptions we make at work that can get in the way of collaboration in teams are:

- Assuming we share the same purpose (individuals may have their own incentives).
- Assuming others share the same views (also known as false consensus bias).
- Assuming we are starting from the same level of understanding (we all come at things from different points of experience).
- Assuming we understand who is responsible for what (role definition can be unique from one person to the next).
- Assuming that no pushback is agreement (silence does not necessarily mean agreement, it can mean it is not safe enough for people to disagree).

That last point led to catastrophic consequences at NASA for both the Challenger crew in 1986 and the Columbia crew in 2003. At the root of the cause of both incidents was a culture of silence – where engineers who knew about technical flaws did not voice their concerns loud enough or with enough insistence to the ultimate decision-makers for fear of making career-limiting moves. Their silence on detected flaws or weakness in the spacecraft designs ultimately led to lost lives and many years of reputation recovery for NASA. Deep inquiry into both incidents revealed that no single individual was to blame – rather a culture of organisational silence that needed to change.

Since then, NASA has undergone deep soul searching and genuine change to culture and leadership practices. One tactic that NASA adopts as common practice to ward against the assumption that silence is agreement, is to end every meeting with the question: *'Is there anything that has not been said that needs to be said?'* This is the way management provide proactive permission to raise concerns or provide a contrary view that could potentially be unpopular. It's an active step towards building a culture of psychological safety and speaking up when there are concerns or issues.

NORMS

Norms are accepted standards or ways of behaving that most people agree with. The 'norm' is also what is considered 'normal' – it's typical of most or the average of the group. Norms are 'how we do things around here'.

Every group has norms – some are explicit norms and some are implicit norms.

Explicit norms are the written rules or expectations that are overtly communicated. We see these in codes of conduct, policies and procedures, laws and regulations, quality standards, contracts and written agreements. These norms are necessary for keeping us safe and harmonious. They are the hallmarks of civilised society whereby adhering to norms and expected standards is both a sign of respect and a way to build trust.

Implicit norms are the unwritten rules about how people are expected to behave. These are not overt – they are communicated via interaction and observation. An example of an implicit cultural norm is the expectation to remove your shoes when entering a household in Japan. Or taking a bottle of wine when invited to dinner. Or sending flowers to commemorate a death in the family. There is no written rule book to these things, every cultural sub-group has their own implicit norms. It is considered a sign of respect to develop cultural awareness and understand the implicit practices of other groups when entering their territory or engaging with them in business.

Where norms can have a negative impact is where the *implicit* expectations do not match the *explicit* expectations.

Many organisations have stated values and norms but very few live them, and this is often because they are not discussed in teams often enough. For example, the organisation may have *respect* as a stated value, but if team members frequently turn up late to meetings, check phones or other devices instead of listening, do not follow-through on actions agreed, or wait until after the meeting to have the 'real conversation', then there is a disconnect between the expectation of respect (the explicit norm) and demonstration of respect (the implicit norm).

When this happens, the explicit norms lose their value and significance. They are empty words on a webpage. They have no meaning because no-one honours them.

The opposite is also true. When people respect the norms and values and demonstrate commitment to adherence of agreed standards, we see cultures of excellence. There is an understanding that all participants are active, there are no passengers, and effort will be both recognised and rewarded.

Norms lead to assumptions. In the example above, if there is a prevailing norm of poor meeting behaviour, this leads to the assumption that meetings are a waste of time. If, conversely, there is a norm of excellence, where people turn up prepared and on time, actively listen, contribute intelligent ideas, and address concerns directly, meetings are productive and an efficient use of time.

In teams, the key to establishing norms is to make the implicit, explicit. To discuss and agree on standards of behaviour for how we each show up. If you want to raise the bar on a 'norm' you need to move from an 'average' expected standard to an 'exceptional' accepted standard. Make high expectations the standard you expect. Be a leader by following through and holding yourself and your teammates accountable to those standards. Be a role model for excellence and ask your teammates to do the same. Recognise when you fall short or make mistakes and use these moments as learning opportunities. Not reasons to admonish or blame, but as reasons to learn.

> **When people respect the norms and values and demonstrate commitment to adherence of agreed standards, we see cultures of excellence.**

SELF-LIMITING BELIEFS

Self-limiting beliefs are false or negative beliefs about ourselves that hold us back and prevent us from fulfilling our potential.

The relationship we have with ourselves is the most important relationship of our lives.

We come into this world with ourselves. We live with ourselves every single day. We die with ourselves. No-one else can join us on the experience of being inside our own minds.

The way we talk to ourselves, the nature of our relationship with ourselves, is the difference between living in a prison of self-imposed limitations, or a sanctuary of freedom and purpose.

> **The way we talk to ourselves, the nature of our relationship with ourselves, is the difference between living in a prison of self-imposed limitations, or a sanctuary of freedom and purpose.**

When we adopt self-limiting beliefs, we come up with limited solutions. The way we talk to ourselves influences the quality of our thinking and the value of our contributions.

This is the difference between a growth mindset and a fixed mindset – a concept introduced by Dr Carol Dweck in her 2006 book *Mindset*.

Dr Dweck is a Stanford University Professor of Psychology who conducted groundbreaking experiments with 10-year-old children when she gave them a challenge that was a little too difficult for them. She noticed a distinct difference between children who kept trying on the task, versus those who just gave up.

Children with a **growth mindset** saw a challenging task as an opportunity to grow and learn. They persisted in the face of setbacks, seeing failures as steps on a learning curve. Children with a **fixed mindset** felt that their core intelligence had been tested and devastated. They were more likely to either run from the next challenge or cheat on the next one. Growth mindset kids see errors as learning opportunities. Fixed mindset kids see errors as evidence of their inherent intelligence and give up trying.

Her research shows a **growth mindset** can be taught and learned. When she taught school children that putting in effort to learn something hard gives our brains a chance to grow, they demonstrated a significant improvement in grade scores compared to children who didn't have that same lesson.

Mindset is everything. It determines how we view the world, how we approach problems, how we experience setbacks and how we relate to others.

By observing my mindset more, I've noticed there are some things I'm fixed on (like my attitude to politicians), and there are some things that I'm more open about (like adaptive technologies). Also, some things I used to be more fixed on I am more open to (like my relationship to debt) and some things I was more open to are becoming more fixed (like my attitude to artwork and music).

A fixed mindset is not fixed, if that makes sense. It all comes down to awareness and being more curious about *why* you believe what you believe. What evidence is there to support your view? Have you questioned the reasons why the opposite view may also be valid?

Self-limiting beliefs are the hallmarks of a fixed mindset. Below is a list of self-limiting beliefs that are examples of a fixed mindset, alongside their growth mindset alternatives.

Self-limiting beliefs of a fixed mindset	Choosing a growth mindset instead
I am no good at...[insert anything]	What I am good at is...
I'm not as good as... [insert anyone]	The strengths I can use here are...
I don't have enough... [time, money, connections, etc]	I have plenty of... [time, money, connections, etc]
I'm not worthy...	I've worked hard for this...
I'm not ready...	I'm going to start with...
I'm not strong/capable enough...	I am enough...
This is too hard for me...	I'm not there, *yet*...
I can't change...	I'm willing to learn...
I'm afraid...	Courage is being afraid and trying it anyway...

If a child was talking to themselves in ways that echo the list on the left, would you pull them up on it? Of course you would! Then why don't we catch ourselves in these unhelpful doom loops of thinking?

The definition of a **belief** is the same as the definition of an assumption – a belief is something you hold to be true, *regardless* of the evidence to support it.

There are no right or wrong beliefs. There are only helpful or unhelpful beliefs. Helpful beliefs are ones that support you to grow. Unhelpful beliefs are those that keep you stuck.

So now that you're aware of the BANS – it's time to BAN the BANS! Learning how to trust yourself to be *unique and independent in thought* is as much about being more aware of when the BANS distort your thinking, as it is about adopting strategies to improve the quality of your thinking. Let's look at these in the next section.

9

Develop independent thinking

'm going to challenge the notion that there is no 'I' in team. I agree that teamwork is only possible when the members work together as a collective, putting egos aside in favour of shared objectives. But the collective can only be high performing when every individual brings their best game.

Teams are made up of individuals. What we don't want is individuals to abdicate themselves to the collective, conforming or compromising on their viewpoints.

Great teams are made up of independent thinkers who contribute ideas not with the intention to sway the group, but to discover the best possible solution together.

Independent thinkers apply rigorous intellectual curiosity to improve the quality of their contributions. To **develop independent thinking,** you need to:

1. **Do your due diligence** – apply rigorous intellectual curiosity to your thinking.

2. **Show up** as your authentic self – share your voice and contribute your perspective.

DO YOUR DUE DILIGENCE

You wouldn't buy a house or a business without first doing due diligence to assess the value of the asset. The same goes for your thinking. Doing your due diligence on your thinking ensures you bring high-quality, high-value ideas to the table.

As part of my business, I run strategic planning workshops with leadership teams to help them align on clear and simple plans to realise shared vision and goals. After working with dozens of teams, I've come to observe that the quality of the output is directly correlated to the quality of thinking done by individuals prior to the day.

To account for this, pre-work is requested by all attendees. The CEO is asked to prepare a presentation including their market assessment, vison for the future, and major opportunities to be realised. The CFO is asked to prepare a trend analysis of revenue and margin over the past five years as well as their predictions for growth over the next five years. All other members are asked to consult their own departments to prepare a SOAR analysis – a positive psychology version of a SWOT – which is an assessment of the company's strengths, opportunities, aspirations and results.

These preparation requirements ensure that each participant comes primed and cognisant of the nuances and complexities of the challenges to growth. This prevents oversimplified ideas or unnecessary debate on the day, and leads to more thoughtful, considered and balanced perspectives shared in the room.

For those who don't do the prep work, it shows. Their ideas are either ill-informed, oversimplified, or actively withheld for fear of being shown up!

Flying by the seat of your pants can get you by in busy moments, but setting aside time for thinking and preparation before working with others to do difficult work goes a long way in fast-tracking to a better outcome.

In addition to the SOAR process mentioned above, here are few more thinking amplifiers for doing your due diligence.

FULL SPECTRUM THINKING

Full spectrum thinking is a concept created by Matt Church and Peter Cook in their 2018 book *Think*. This book was written for thought leaders – people who want to commercialise their IP (intellectual property) by being known for knowing something. But it is equally useful for anyone wanting to improve their critical thinking skills.

Full spectrum thinking encourages us to flesh out an idea by scoping it from multiple perspectives: from left brain (logical, rational) to right brain (creative, emotional), and from conceptual (big picture, theoretical) down to concrete (specific, contextual).

Church and Cook came up with what they call a 'Pink Sheet'[1] – essentially a template to capture an idea from each quadrant that results from a 2×2 matrix. They called it a Pink Sheet because it was accidentally printed on a pink piece of paper – and the name stuck!

Full spectrum thinking asks you to scope out a single concept by thinking about:

- A model or framework that explains it: conceptual, left brain quadrant.

- A metaphor that gives it a reference point: conceptual, right brain quadrant.

- Research or data to support it: concrete, left brain quadrant.

- Stories or quotes that bring it to life: concrete, right brain quadrant.

Here's an example of how I've applied full spectrum thinking to a concept in this book (see Chapter 7):

- **Idea:** Thoughts don't come *to* you, they come *though* you.

- **Model:** Circular flow chart.

- **Metaphor:** Hardware and software.

---

1   The Pink Sheet template is freely available at https://thoughtleaders.com.au/ pink-sheets-process/

- **Data and fact:** Dr Michael Muthukrishna's book *A Theory of Everyone*.

- **Story:** *So You Think You Can Dance* TV show.

Applying this method to thinking is a useful way of sifting a concept or idea through your own lens and adding value by adding a variation, extending it, or applying it to a new context.

YES AND, YES BUT

This is another thinking amplifier shared by Church and Cook in *Think*. When you hear a concept or idea that you either agree or disagree with, use this method to *build upon* the idea with your unique perspective.

'*Yes, and*' asks you to elaborate on why you agree with an idea or concept, or how it could play out in your specific context.

'*Yes, but*' asks you to find the evidence to support the opposing idea, challenge the idea, highlight what's missing, or provide a contrary view.

Yes is different to *No*. *Yes* suggests we are building concepts. *No* suggests we are debating concepts. *Yes and*, and *Yes but* creates a dynamic in which a paradox can exist. This is important if we are going to create new solutions to existing problems.

A paradox is a situation in which opposing concepts can both be true. There is a paradox presented in Chapter 7.

'*There are no more truly original ideas.*'

AND

'*We are all unique and independent in thought.*'

How can these two statements both be true?

My answer to this paradox is that humans both download from, and upload to, the 'cloud' of human knowledge, filtering our ideas through our own unique values, experiences and preferences.

Paradoxes are often at the centre of problems being solved in leadership teams:

- How can we grow both revenue and margin at the same time?
- How can we drive up both productivity and engagement?
- How can we reduce our headcount and improve wellbeing?
- How can we gain market share and consolidate our offerings?
- How can we simplify our operations and expand into new regions?
- How can we strengthen data security and maintain agile systems?
- How can we minimise our climate footprint and maintain our costs?

These questions are paradoxical until they are considered from different angles, with an intention to build on ideas, not debate them. *Yes, and* or *Yes, but* are useful ways to contribute options to conversations without de-valuing an alternate viewpoint and missing out on potentially new, creative ways of solving these dilemmas.

SCIENTIFIC THINKING

The main premise behind scientific thinking is to treat opinions and ideas as hypotheses to be tested as either true or not true – as opposed to statements of irrefutable fact.

The whole design of the scientific method is to ward against cognitive biases like confirmation bias getting in the way of the truth. While it's very difficult to completely remove bias,[1] the whole point about testing assumptions and questions through research is to be open to the fact that you might be wrong, and that being proven wrong is still a result!

---

1   **Confirmation bias** can occur when researchers look for patterns in the data to confirm the idea or opinion they hold. **Selection bias** occurs when researchers select participants into study and control groups instead of randomly assigning them. **Publishing bias** is not publishing findings of null results because they are perceived as less interesting, which can skew our understanding of the topic. **Observation bias** can occur when participants are aware they are being observed by a scientist and alter the way they act or respond either consciously or unconsciously.

There are three possible answers to all scientific research questions:

1. P > .05 is really exciting. It proves a strong correlation between factor X and factor Y. For example, I've proved there is a strong correlation between curiosity and learning.

2. P > .01 is a weak, yet still significant correlation. It indicates I'm on the right track. I've proved there is a relationship between curiosity and learning, but it needs further testing.

3. P = 0 is a null result. I've proved there is no correlation between curiosity and learning beyond chance. This can initially feel disappointing, but a null result is still a result!

Being OK with being proved wrong is a *big part* of adopting a scientific approach to thinking.

> **Being OK with being proved wrong is a *big part* of adopting a scientific approach to thinking.**

For workers, adopting a scientific approach to thinking is about being willing to test ideas and let them go when they don't work out.

The smart people at Google X have designed a whole innovation factory around scientific thinking. They call it The Moonshot Factory. Google X is a diverse group of inventors and entrepreneurs who build and launch technologies that aim to deliver a 10x impact on the world's most intractable problems. They are the team behind self-driving cars, self-flying delivery vehicles, smart glasses, smart contact lenses and balloon-powered internet. To give themselves the freedom to move fast, they try to kill as many projects as possible, as early as possible. The idea is that they want to move quickly from idea to prototype and fail fast if it doesn't work. Only 3% of projects make it to the second stage, and only half again are expected to survive.

Team X have created a culture where failure is normalised and even celebrated. They see failure as a positive, because in the words of one of their employees, 'killing a good idea, makes room for truly great ones'.

DESIGN THINKING

In 2004, business consultants Hasso Plattner and David Kelley introduced a revolutionary model that transformed problem-solving approaches for engineers, designers, and eventually educators, business leaders, and social entrepreneurs everywhere. They called it the Human Centered Design Process, or in short, design thinking.

This innovative approach encourages individuals to identify and tackle problems through three unconventional ways:

1. **Empathise** – understand the problems and challenges from the perspective of the 'user' or customer.

2. **Work together** – recognise that creativity sparks from collaboration – that working together can and does produce a better result than individuals working alone.

3. **Fail effectively** – work fast to build a minimum viable product (MVP) and test it. Adopt a 'fail fast' mentality, seeing continuous improvement, or iterative improvement over perfection.

Plattner and Kelley brought the Human Centered Design (HCD) method to the forefront by developing IDEO, an international product design firm, and the Stanford Design School. The design method is characterised by five steps, as pictured below:

Design Thinking Method

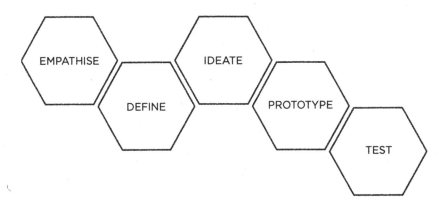

Design thinking is a process that extends far beyond the context of traditional design. It is a process that can be applied to the way individuals and teams think to solve existing problems or innovate entirely new solutions. In fact, design thinking has been identified as a key process for Australian leaders and boards to adopt when it comes to leading and governing organisations.

Catherine Livingstone is the Chancellor of the University of Technology Sydney (UTS) and director of multiple boards including The Australian Ballet and Australian Design Council. As the keynote speaker at the 2024 AICD Australian Governance Summit she advocated that business leaders adopt design thinking. She said:

> 'I fear that Australia has a blind spot when it comes to the value of design and design thinking. We tend to think of it only in the context of a product or fashion, but it is so much deeper and extends to service design, software design, process design, value chain design, business model design – and strategy design. And dare I say, policy design.'[1]

Applying design thinking helps teams quickly evolve their thinking to respond to feedback and improve their work. For example, I used design thinking to help an executive team in a strategy creation workshop. First, I drew this diagram up on the flipchart:

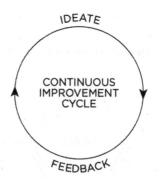

In the workshop, two sub-groups worked on separate aspects of the vision (one was defining their fly-wheel, the other was defining their

---

1   Reported on the AICD website: https://www.aicd.com.au/good-governance/aicd-australian-governance-summit-2024-at-the-forefront.html

growth factors). In each round, one sub-group presented their ideas, and the other provided feedback. They went back to their respective corners of the room to keep working on their concepts, massaging them based on the insights and reactions they received. We continued this process for as many rounds as was needed to eventually land on concepts and ideas that everyone could agree with (in reality, this took only two rounds). This process led to rapid buy-in, iteration and improvement, without the need to defend or get bogged down in unnecessary details.

Design thinking is a great method for improving the way individuals come up with and test ideas by working collaboratively with others.

DE BONO'S HATS

A chapter on thinking methods would not be complete without honouring the amazing Edward De Bono and his incredible contribution to the field of thinking and creativity. There is no way I can do justice to his life's work in just a few short paragraphs, but I hope that at least reading these lines might pique your interest to follow up his methods and techniques yourself.

Perhaps the most popular of all De Bono's thinking tools are his six hats. The idea is that to avoid thinking diminishers like cognitive biases, assumptions and norms, we should consider an idea from different perspectives – weighing the pros and cons of all options. This, De Bono suggests, is an effective way to overcome the challenges of being locked in two-sided arguments. His method has helped solve deep tensions experienced in highly unionised environments, political conflicts, corporate impasses, hung juries, and disaster relief efforts.

The hats represent six different ways of thinking in parallel to explore a subject in a constructive and not adversarial way. The idea is that all people working on the problem put the same hat on at the same time; considering the problem from all angles together. The premise is that when they change perspective and put themselves on the other side of the argument for a moment, they are able to see solutions that didn't appear before, because they were previously locked in defending a single perspective.

The hats are:

- **Blue – the facilitator (organising and controlling) hat.** It's used at the front of the discussion to decide on the focus and what sequence of hats to use. The chairperson or facilitator of the discussion wears this hat throughout so that they may bring people back on track should they stray to a different hat. At the end the blue hat is used for the outcome, summary and next steps.

- **White – the information and data hat.** What is the reality of the situation? The facts, the data, the things that are already known.

- **Red – the feelings, emotion and intuition hat.** This hat gives space to the emotions on the topic and allows participants' experiences to be acknowledged and observed.

- **Black – the critical thinking hat.** What are the negatives to the problem or idea being discussed. What are the risks and dangers?

- **Yellow – the positive hat.** Consider the positives, benefits, potential sources of value to the problem or idea being discussed.

- **Green – the creative hat.** What are some options? What ideas are there to solve? What other alternatives and possibilities are there?

While in business we may not always have the time to wear all the hats for every idea or discussion, this concept is useful to bring in anytime I observe a team locked in debate. By simply saying, 'How about we all wear the green hat for a while', I can prompt people to switch into a different mode of thinking and help unlock more productive discussions.

This is by no means an exhaustive list of thinking methods but these are the ones I've used in my own practice and had most success with. I've seen them have significant impact both on my own thinking, and on the way leaders and leadership teams approach their work.

Of course, there is no use just working on how you think if you're not willing to share your thoughts with others. Let's understand why showing up is just as important as doing our due diligence when it comes to developing independent thinking.

10

Show up

Independent thinking can only add value when we are brave enough to show up as our authentic selves. To be a high-performing team, we need strong individual contributors.

Showing up is about so much more than just clocking on.

It's listening with an open mind and then tapping into your own knowledge and experiences so that you can add value to the problems being discussed and solved. When we say 'dig deep' we often mean digging further into your experiences – going past the comfortable and obvious to the vulnerable and unique.

SHOW UP FOR YOURSELF – LISTEN TO YOUR VOICE

To show up for yourself, you need to tap into your emotions.

So many leaders think that a sign of strength is not 'getting emotional' or 'letting emotions cloud reason'. But the reality is, your emotions are part of every decision you make, whether you're aware of them or not. Deep within your psyche, your values are colouring how you feel about everything you experience, because they are based on what you've learned before. Emotions are data that provide valuable information. In fact, without access to them, our effectiveness can be significantly challenged.

Phineas Gage is a famous test case for the crippling effects of losing our emotions in reasoning. Phineas Gage was the unfortunate victim of an accident in the 1800s when, while building a train track, an explosion sent a pole straight through his pre-frontal cortex. Remarkably, he not only survived, but he was also able to walk out of hospital after a few months of recovery, seemingly unaffected. Until the strangest thing started to happen.

The accident had not affected his ability to think, plan or reason. What it had done was disconnect his thinking centres from his limbic or emotion centres. He could no longer use emotions to guide decisions. Every decision became a labour of weighing pros and cons and he became paralysed with decision overload. Simple tasks such as choosing what to wear, what to eat or what to do with his day would take hours. He couldn't keep down a job and eventually all his relationships broke down including those with his wife and children. Poor Phineas was a test case in neuroscience that has since been observed and validated through fMRI imaging in similar injuries.

The message is clear, emotions are not just useful data, they are essential components in critical thinking and reasoning; and they are in fact the definitive difference between AI and human judgement. Machines don't have feelings. Humans do.

Building emotional intelligence starts with letting yourself feel the feels. Instead of blocking or denying your emotions, be curious about them. Being curious about your emotions was an idea first mentioned back in Chapter 6 as a way of changing your relationship to the discomfort of learning.

Instead of dismissing or ignoring emotions, use them as fuel to find the experiences from your past that add value to a conversation or decision-making process. Develop your emotional intelligence by asking yourself three simple questions each time you're processing your thoughts or ideas:

- What do I think?
- Why is this significant?
- What emotion do I attach to it?

These three little questions provide a check-in mechanism. By asking yourself not just what you *think* but how you *feel* and *why* that is important, you're giving yourself permission to let your unique experiences add value to the conversation. When practiced regularly, it is a habit that can dramatically improve your emotional intelligence and capability to lead both yourself and others in any team context.

> **Instead of dismissing or ignoring emotions, use them as fuel to find the experiences from your past that add value to a conversation or decision-making process.**

SHOW UP FOR THE TEAM - SHARE YOUR VOICE

Showing up for the team means taking ultimate accountability for the part you play in the team culture and their ultimate success. We can only do this by sharing our authentic experience.

Being authentic is the opposite of masking. It's being honest and transparent – being willing to challenge norms, recognise where bias clouds judgement, identify unhelpful assumptions or help people see past self-limiting beliefs.

There is no doubt that good-quality thinking comes out of diversity of ideas. If your idea or opinion is different to the norm, it takes courage to share it, but it's what ultimately adds value and is, in fact, what you're hired to do!

I often see this behaviour in people starting out in their leadership careers. They demonstrate approval seeking, dependence and conventionalism. That is – they are keen to fit in and show their support for their superiors by sharing the popular opinion, or the opinion that they believe most others will either like or approve of. This is not helpful in their roles as emerging leaders. Leaders stand out from the crowd, lead change, and challenge existing norms and assumptions that no longer serve the business. Leaders take the interpersonal risk necessary to make an impact, not concerning themselves with fitting in but rather expanding the way people think about problems and find new solutions to organisational challenges.

I have been running the Future Leaders Program for a scaleup in the travel industry in Australia for three consecutive years. As part of the program, the candidates prepare and deliver a 'shark tank' presentation to their executive by sharing a new idea for a way to significantly impact the business. The best ideas are supported with funding and resources to implement. The program is successful in elevating careers – at least 50% of graduates from this program are promoted within 12 months of completion. The very notion of this program is to encourage participants to innovate, challenge the norm and think differently.

Sharing your voice is not only essential to leading teams and creating change, it is an essential component to driving your own career growth and improving your earning capacity.

A LION, A SHEEP, A TURTLE AND A CAMEL WALK INTO A BAR...

No, this is not the opening sentence of a bad joke. But it is a fun way to make a serious point!

If we turn independent thinking into a 2×2 matrix with 'due diligence' along the horizontal, and 'showing up' along the vertical, we get four animals.

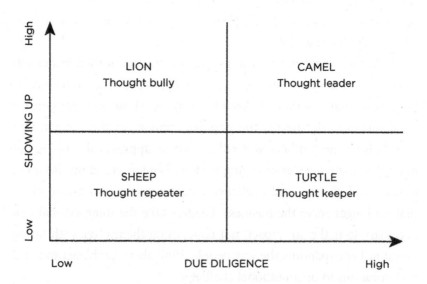

Sheep are thought repeaters. They are afflicted with conformity bias – applying little to no testing of whatever the predominant view is in the group. They only speak up when asked to, and when they do it's to repeat the prevailing idea in the group at the time. Sheep are common in new starters who are keen to fit in, or in cultures where it is either not safe or pointless to challenge authority. Wherever there are sheep, there are lions, because lions feed off sheep.

Lions are thought bullies. They are all too willing to share their opinions, regardless of their expertise or authority to do so. Lions beat their opponents down with the 'proof' of their worldview, fed back to them by algorithms that strengthen their conformation bias. They can be intellectually lazy, sharing opinions that are rarely tested or validated for the truth. They seek out sheep because they live off the validation their conformity bias provides.

Turtles are thought keepers. They are very wise, having moved slowly and mindfully though the vicissitudes of life and taken time to contemplate their experience. Living close to the ground, they take a detailed view of the world and are constantly curious about the world in front of them. However, they don't much enjoy being challenged, especially by lions, and so retreat often into their shells especially when threatened or tired. Getting them to come out of their shells takes considerable effort – it needs to be completely safe and there can't be any lions prowling about.

Camels are thought leaders. They are persistent, unwavering and self-reliant. They survive the harshest environments and are willing to learn the best way to survive through testing, learning and shaping what they know. They are anything but nice – not afraid to show up and share their view whether it be popular or unpopular. They also understand that working as a team is necessary to survival, but that each one must pull their weight. Camels carry everyone else's baggage – they pave the way for commerce, connecting cultures and creating opportunities for their masters. But it's not all about the destination. For camels, it's also about enjoying the journey and going at their own pace.

It is no secret that I am a big fan of camels! A camel once saved my husband's life after he was struck by a scorpion in the Saharan desert and needed to be carried across treacherously steep sand dunes to the nearest village for anti-venom. When I was thinking about the perfect symbol for my business – a business about helping leaders sustain high performance in challenging environments – the camel was the obvious choice and is proudly represented in my company logo.

To be a camel, leaders do the work of developing their capacity for independent thought by applying rigorous intellectual curiosity, and showing up as their most authentic self. This takes effort, persistence and courage, but the reward is that you get to cross vast distances, experience extraordinary lands, and encounter all kinds of interesting people along the way.

Part II summary

- To stay relevant in the age of AI and smart machines, we need to develop the uniquely human skills of creative thinking, analytical thinking, self-management and curiosity.

- Thinking is a premium, and yet it is also the very thing that is most at risk.

- In modern times, we are facing a triple threat to quality thinking including algorithms, attention theft and burnout.
  - Algorithms reinforce biases.
  - Attention theft robs us of time.
  - Burnout robs us of energy.

- Curiosity is an essential quality of high-performing teams because it is the antidote to the triple threat of algorithms, attention theft and burnout.
  - Curiosity is a source of resilience to stress by giving us the psychological space necessary to choose a constructive response.
  - Curiosity feeds learning because it puts us into a state of inquiry – and allows us to tolerate ambiguity for the time it takes to find the joy of discovery.
  - Curiosity sparks creativity. Being more open to different viewpoints can lead to new ideas that drive innovation.

- To be curious, we need to develop independent thinking. High-performing teams need independent thinkers. Not co-dependent repeaters.

- Thoughts don't come *to* you, they come *though* you. Humans both download from, and upload to, the 'cloud' of human knowledge, adding value by building on or altering concepts in our own way.

- You are unique and independent in thought because your lens of the world is coloured by your unique combination of values, attributes and experiences.

- Projection is the unconscious process of psychologically transmitting thoughts and feelings to others in ways that make them perceive them as their own. We often project what we can't contain (e.g. uncomfortable emotions).

  - Gaslighting is projecting nasty feelings of worthlessness, doubt, fear and shame on the same target over and over until that individual questions their own perception of reality.

  - The Pygmalion effect occurs when others rise or fall to the level of our expectations. What we expect of others creates a self-fulfilling prophecy where they believe the same of themselves.

- The BANS are cognitive shortcuts our brains use to minimise processing effort. These are biases, assumptions, norms and self-limiting beliefs. We need to BAN the BANS!

  - Biases are prejudices towards or against something or someone. Confirmation bias is the bias that algorithms and marketing campaigns play into the most.

  - Assumptions are things you accept as true without question or proof. Assumptions make an ASS out of U and ME!

  - Norms are accepted standards of behaviour that most people agree with and conform to.

  - Self-limiting beliefs are false or negative beliefs we hold about ourselves that hold us back or prevent us from fulfilling our potential.

- Great teams are made up of independent thinkers who contribute ideas not with the intention to sway the group, but to discover the best possible solution together.

- Independent thinkers apply rigorous intellectual curiosity to improve the quality of their contributions. To develop independent thinking, you need to:

  - **Do your due diligence** – apply rigorous intellectual curiosity to your thinking.

- **Show up** as your authentic self – share your voice and contribute your perspective.
- Due diligence strategies ensure we assess the value of our ideas and thoughts. They include:
  - **Full spectrum thinking** – scoping a concept from left brain (logical) to right brain (emotional), and from concept (big picture) to the concrete (specific detail).
  - *Yes and*, and *Yes but* – is asking you to consider how you agree with or disagree with a concept, extending it 'in your own words'.
  - **Scientific thinking** – is about seeing your ideas as hypotheses to be tested, and being OK with being proven wrong.
  - **Design thinking** – is about tackling problems with empathy, collaboration and iteration. It involves adopting a 'fail fast' mentality to continuous improvement with regular cycles of ideation and feedback.
  - **De Bono's hats** – are about considering an idea from multiple perspectives, including the facts, the benefits, the problems, the emotions and the alternatives.
- Independent thinking can only add value when we are brave enough to show up as our authentic selves.
  - **To show up for ourselves** – we need to listen to our own voice.
  - **To show up for others** – we need to share our view.
- When we combine *due diligence* with *showing up* in a 2×2 matrix, we get four types of thinkers.
  - **Sheep** are low on due diligence and low on showing up. They are thought repeaters.
  - **Lions** are low on due diligence but high on showing up. They are thought bullies.
  - **Turtles** are high on due diligence, but low on showing up. They are thought keepers.

- **Camels** are high on due diligence and high on showing up. They are thought leaders.

• High-performing teams need thought leaders – people who develop their capacity for independent thought by applying rigorous intellectual curiosity, and showing up as their most authentic self.

Part III

Be Connected

'Vulnerability is the birthplace of innovation, creativity and change.'

Brené Brown

11

Everything is connected

Liz Ritchie is the CEO of the Regional Australia Institute (RAI), an independent policy think-tank and research organisation dedicated to growth of opportunity in regional and rural Australia. I first met Ritchie in 2008 when we were both mature-age students returning to university to complete our Masters of Organisation Dynamics. We took an instant liking to one another and stayed in contact over the years. When she stepped in to lead the RAI, she knew her training in systems dynamics was going to come in handy. She reached out to me in 2024 to work with her leadership team and help them achieve what she knew was going to be a big ambition. While briefing me for the project, Ritchie shared with me her story of how she and her team at the RAI were leading policy change that would dramatically change the prospects for Australians living in rural and regional communities.

Ritchie knows that if regions are stronger, Australia prospers. She also knows that her organisation's voice alone is not enough to realise the large-scale systemic change necessary to make a lasting impact on the prognosis for regional economies.

'There was a growing level of frustration about the issues impacting regional Australia. So regional people called for a collectively designed vision and plan. A North star, or driving purpose, that aligned the vast array of intersecting issues and interests of regional Australia and provided the systemic platform we needed,' she told me.

Following extensive work and consultation the RAI spearheaded a massive effort to combine forces with public, private, government and NFP organisations, all with a vested interest in regional prosperity to build a shared ambition. Over two years of applied effort, they built the *Regionalisation Ambition 2032 – a Framework to Rebalance the Nation* to drive regional growth involving collaborative action from multiple stakeholders. It involved a massive consultation effort including 2000+ individuals from over 150 organisations and all levels of government.

Spanning five pillars, the Regionalisation Ambition is underpinned by 20 targets addressing fundamental aspects of regional living. If achieved, these targets will improve the lives of regional Australians for generations to come and, importantly, create a better Australia.

Ritchie and her team ran workshops across regional centres that involved a variety of key stakeholders who each brought a different perspective to the discussion.

'Our number one co-designers were our committed members, because they too shared our vision and our values,' she told me. 'Government was a slower burn because, on the one hand, they want to be part of the process, on the other, they are often risk averse.' She also sought the voices of organisations who weren't members but important groups with a footprint in regional Australia such as the Royal Flying Doctor Service, National Farmers Federation, National Rural Health Alliance and the Australian Rural Leadership Foundation to name a few. This cohort later became instrumental in formatting a further advocacy group called the National Alliance for Regionalisation, encompassing 35+ peak organisations who want to drive the Ambition forward.

'The work required deep systems thinking in order to galvanize any kind of change. The reason traction was slow is because this is a big wicked challenge and many big, wicked challenges are impossible to deal with without creating a systems approach.'

'Wicked' challenges are such because they involve a tangled web of problems for which there are multiple stakeholders, no single identifiable cause, no precedent, and no way of evaluating whether any single remedy will work. The design theorists Horst Rittel and Melvin Webber first introduced the term 'wicked problem' in 1973 to draw attention to the complexities and challenges of addressing planning and social policy programs. Wicked challenges are complex and require systems thinking to solve. Poverty, homelessness, domestic violence, terrorism, and climate change are all examples of wicked problems.

Regionalisation is a wicked problem – because you cannot drive regional economic growth without also addressing housing, education, skills, health, infrastructure and environmental factors. For this reason, the Regionalisation Framework invites regional organisations to make pledges that facilitate any of five pillars that support regional growth: population, jobs and skills, liveability, productivity and innovation, and sustainability and resilience.

As Ritchie told me:

> 'I was on repeat about working with the coalition of the willing. We were the architects, not the owners for the Regionalisation Ambition. The ambition to rebalance the nation is owned by the movement. By leaning into systems thinking, leveraging collective intelligence, and enabling collaborative action we almost became the container or holding yard for the mobilisation of good. This entire movement was based on strength-based principles. It's about having ambition, aspiration, hope and optimism all rolled into one.'

Should the RAI and their collaborators be successful in stewarding the Regionalisation Ambition to achieve more balanced population growth across regional and city centres, they will deliver a substantial impact on the Australian economy. Scenario modelling by the National Institute of Economic and Industry Research[1] predicts that should the high regional population growth be achieved (where regional populations account for 11 million of the national total), Australia's total national output will reach $2297 trillion. That's **$13.8 billion more**

---

1   Reported in *Regionalisation Ambition 2032: A Framework to Rebalance the Nation*, p.11.

than the total national output under organic or 'business as usual' regional population growth.

To keep the nation accountable, the RAI committed to reporting annually on progress against 20 targets that address fundamental aspects of regional living, captured in the five pillars of the framework. In 2023, one year in, they observed several target measures in education, migration and sustainability moving in the right direction, while several target measures were lagging – particularly in recruitment difficulty and housing availability.

Ritchie maintains an optimistic view.

> 'The complexity is so vast that we need to think long-term. We are really conscious when we launch a progress report that we're leading with the positives and highlighting areas where we need to double our focus. No single agency can solve this alone. It is only through sharing and learning from this work that we can build the momentum required to lead a whole of system change.'

For organisations like the RAI, being connected is about more than just tapping into the collective intelligence of a team. It's about tapping into the collective intelligence of a system.

To think systemically is to appreciate that everything is connected. Instead of viewing things in linear cause-and-effect ways, system thinking invites us to acknowledge and appreciate the intricate web of relationships and feedback loops that influence outcomes. We are individuals, working in teams, interacting in an organisation, within a marketplace, in an economy, in a geo-political context, on planet Earth.

> **Instead of viewing things in linear cause-and-effect ways, system thinking invites us to acknowledge and appreciate the intricate web of relationships and feedback loops that influence outcomes.**

In business, systems thinking encourages us to appreciate how market dynamics emerge through the many interactions of individuals working in teams, in organisations, and to look for patterns across these entities that influence outcomes, rather than trying to over-simplify what are inherently complex problems.

Let's explore how systems thinking can enhance teamwork and positively impact performance.

TAP INTO THE SYSTEM

One of the major advantages to systems thinking is its potential to foster collaboration and cooperation. When we recognise that no single individual or entity has all the answers, we become open to engaging with diverse perspectives and expertise. By bringing together people with diverse views, we can collectively explore complex issues and co-create innovative solutions.

Connected teams tap into the system. Every team member's experience is a valid data point – together they provide a more complete picture. Individual thoughts and feelings are different representations 'of the system', allowing us to view challenges and opportunities more holistically.

When light passes through rain, it splits into the seven different colours of the rainbow. The same happens in teams. When a team is presented with a new issue, problem or opportunity, it splits into different perspectives. Each different perspective sheds light on the issue, opening a window that is unique.

CREATE SHARED VALUE

The second major advantage to thinking systemically is that it is more sustainable – both for business and for the world.

When teams adopt a systems approach to thinking they broaden their consideration of their sphere of influence to include the impact their decisions will have on the system of stakeholders. They consider both short-term and long-term implications for decisions, asking themselves: 'Is it sustainable?' 'Is it inclusive?' 'How does this benefit each stakeholder group?' This filter enables leaders to delay short-term gratification for long-term reward. This allows them to see the bigger picture, and to understand how their contributions have the potential to create a legacy of value.

Conscious capitalism is a global movement of business leaders and thought leaders who see business as a force for good. Not as a destructive force in pursuit of profits at all costs – but as a healing force, integrating the needs of all stakeholders in the pursuit of shared value creation. The conscious capitalist movement was founded by Raj Sisodia, Distinguished Professor of Global Business at Babson College in the US, and John Mackey, Whole Foods Co-founder, as a new way of doing business – one that appreciates and even respects the interconnectedness of all things.

Conscious capitalists think systemically. They approach business as a vehicle to shared wealth and value creation among all stakeholders by putting purpose at the centre of business strategy. A clear higher purpose – a purpose beyond profit or reason for being that adds value to customers – is a motivating force that aligns and engages all members of the organisation's community.

What's more, the pursuit of higher purpose in a conscious business comes not at a cost to any single stakeholder group, but in pursuit of shared value creation for all. This means balancing and integrating the needs of all stakeholders – investors, partners, employees, suppliers, community and the environment.

As it turns out, being a purpose-driven company pays off in ways that far surpass expectations. Raj Sisodia teamed up with Jag Sheath and David Wolfe to research the financial performance of a sample of conscious companies – companies who actively pursued a higher purpose while integrating and balancing the needs of all stakeholders. This included companies like Patagonia, Disney, 3M, Southwest Airlines, BMW, Toyota, Unilever, IKEA and Novo Nordisk. Raj and his colleagues anticipated the firms they researched would demonstrate at least equal performance to the industry average. Instead, conscious firms outperformed the overall stock market by a ratio of 10.5:1 over a 15-year period, delivering more than 1600% total returns compared to the market average of 150% for the same period.

The growing movement of purpose-driven companies are finding voice through organisations like B Corp and 1% for the Planet. Investors are also paying more attention to purpose-driven companies. Richard Branson's daughter, Holly Branson, is the Chief Purpose and Vision Officer at Virgin. In response to a question posted on her father's blog about what makes a start-up stand out for investment, Holly responded: 'When we look for a new start-up to invest in, we really look for sustainable businesses that are driven by strong purpose to make the world a better place and use innovation to drive this forward.'

Systems thinking can be a superpower. To adopt a systems approach is to understand that on a fundamental level, everything is connected, and that our experiences, feelings and thoughts are data points that inform us about what is going on in the system. If harnessed in teams, it has the potential to broaden the scope of perceptions and experiences considered, and it also allows members to consider the implications of their choices beyond an immediate monetary gain.

Systems thinking can be a superpower.

CONNECTEDNESS IS A STRENGTH

Is 'connectedness' a skill that can be developed?

The folks at Gallup seem to think so. They have researched and developed a diagnostic tool called the Clifton StrengthsFinder that measures 34 different character strengths – or inherent talents that humans universally are born with to varying degrees – and which can become our strengths with the investment of knowledge, skill and practice.

'Connectedness' is one of 34 different strengths they've identified in their research. It is itself a measurable and classified talent for understanding the links between all things. People strong in connectedness are adept at building communities, finding commonalities, helping others see how their efforts fit into a larger picture, and breaking down silos.

While some are born with a greater propensity for connectedness, it can be developed and mastered with the right skills and knowledge – just like any universal human talent.

To be more connected, we need to learn the principles and practices to leverage the shared pool of talent and resources, available whenever groups of people come together to serve a shared purpose.

As we shall read in the next chapter, to be more connected, you need start with building two fundamental human values – trust and respect.

12

The bonds that tie

In all relationships there are two essential ingredients that must be present for the relationship to flourish. These are mutual trust and mutual respect.

Where there is trust and respect, individuals have clarity on goals, roles and responsibilities, and how their parts work together as a whole. Team members are enabled to bring their full self, confident that their efforts will align with the efforts of their teammates and will translate to results. Self-interest is second to serving the interest of the group, because serving the group *is* serving the self. There is mutual benefit to self and others in connected teams.

When trust is broken, or when there is disrespect, teams are disconnected and fragmented. In disconnected teams, individuals focus on self-preservation. The team dynamic becomes dysfunctional, characterised by confrontation, compromise or conformity. Trust can be built, but only through tolerance, courage and vulnerability.

In my practice, I work with leaders and leadership teams to reconnect by strengthening bonds of trust and respect so that they may leverage collective capability. The following case study is a typical example of a dysfunctional team, who worked together to improve their dynamic.

The CEO of a global software engineering company reached out to me after several years of challenging results. We made a time to meet, at his office, in a newly appointed office building in the suburbs of Melbourne. This company had been in operation for almost 50 years. They had a strong brand and solid reputation as a leader in their industry. They had grown to over 500 employees, with operations across Australia, Asia and Europe. The CEO was well dressed in a suit and tie, and ushered me in for what was to be a very honest conversation. He shared with me that while the company had demonstrated consistent steady growth in the past, their rate of growth was slowing and margins were deteriorating. The atmosphere was getting tense in executive team meetings. He did not want to downsize his team or his organisation as a solution to the margin problem – in their industry, talent was hard to find and harder to keep. But he wanted revenue growth and this meant a paradigm shift to the leadership team's way of operating.

Together we planned a strategy retreat for two nights in a coastal town, one hour south of Melbourne. It was the middle of winter and we found a venue on the Mornington Peninsula with a room that had a fireplace and views of a rugged sea. This dramatic setting was the perfect change of pace from their day-to-day office experience.

Prior to the retreat, I met individually with members of his executive team to understand their perspectives. It became apparent that their greatest challenge was an absence of trust. They admitted they were perceived by their direct reports as overly results focussed, prone to setting unrealistic and unattainable goals, and lacking empathy. Each executive team member felt dissatisfied with their performance and had little faith in their peers' capabilities to overcome the challenges facing the group.

One executive shared with me that in previous years it had been fun to be in the executive team. But somewhere along the way, things changed. Competition increased. Sales were harder to land. They were chasing quarterly results, with no clear longer-term vision. They were mentally tired of putting up a fight, spending time and energy justifying their position instead of addressing the problems that needed to be solved.

If they were to overcome this challenging dynamic, they needed to face it. So, in our retreat, I held up the metaphoric mirror. On the display were these words:

crucify, grenade, war room, tear each other apart, fight to the death, pick your battles, sink or swim, on your own, hung out to dry, thrown under the bus.

'These are the words you used to describe what it feels like to be in this team,' I said.

No-one spoke. This was the very thing they had been avoiding. It did not feel safe in this group. Their dynamic was not healthy and yet to address it required vulnerability to speak up. The protracted silence was finally broken when one of the executives expressed his feelings.

'I don't want it to feel like that,' he said. 'I want it to feel like it did when we were having fun.'

In this small act of courage, this individual simultaneously acknowledged the absence of trust and took the first step towards rebuilding it. His vulnerability opened the door for others to follow. Vulnerability is the first necessary step towards rebuilding trust.

What followed was a day spent solely focussed on openly discussing the dynamic of the group and how each individual could take responsibility for changing it. Everyone asked for frank and fearless feedback from each colleague on how they could be better. Everyone listened, heard what was said, and thanked their peers for their honesty.

The first to ask for feedback was the CEO. He made himself vulnerable by admitting to his own faults and demonstrating that he was open to any comments his executives were willing to share – including their criticism. He paved the way for others to do the same. One by one, the walls between them started to crumble and there was a palpable shift in the openness and willingness of the group to share their real concerns and fears about the business and their capacity to lead through its difficult moment. We created the circle of trust – an explicit agreement outlining their principles for working together. This moment led to a tangible shift in their team dynamic.

By stepping into vulnerability, the executive team reformed bonds of trust and respect that allowed them to reset their vision and shift the culture of their business towards a more balanced view of people and performance. This shift has endured in the 10 years since. While executive team members have moved on and new members have joined in that time, the CEO has maintained the importance of creating these moments in their annual calendar where the team revive their circle of trust. Each year he invites me back to open the circle and invite members to give and receive feedback in ways that enables them to stay connected and aligned. This practice has seen this group achieve a rate of growth that has outpaced their previous eight years, even with COVID in the middle of that period.

Trust and respect are the bonds that tie. They are the essential glue that hold people in healthy relationship dynamics.

> **Trust and respect are the bonds that tie. They are the essential glue that hold people in healthy relationship dynamics.**

Trust is essential to vulnerability. Trust and vulnerability go hand in hand. To trust is to be vulnerable, and to be vulnerable is to trust. Both are essential to getting at the real concerns, real viewpoints and diversity of views essential to effective problem solving and ultimate buy-in.

Respect is essential to showing up. Respect ensures we appreciate differences. When we show respect, we acknowledge and invite the full scope of thinking in the room. We withhold judgement, and instead seek to understand others' perspectives.

When trust is broken, or when there is disrespect, teams are disconnected and fragmented. Without these tandem ties, there will only ever be surface sub-standard ideas and appetite for low-level risks. This leads to average and disappointing results.

Let's explore how the bonds of trust and respect play a part in building high-performing teams.

THE BOND OF TRUST

As we learned back in Chapter 2, the absence of trust is the first of Lencioni's five dysfunctions of a team. Creating a foundation of trust is a prerequisite for teams to be open to different points of view and to constructively deal with conflict. Without trust, it is very difficult to 'get to the heart of the matter'. Trust is essential to creating a psychologically safe environment where it is safe to own up to a mistake, share a dissenting or unpopular idea, express uncertainty, or ask for help.

Trust, psychological safety, and vulnerability are inextricably linked. One cannot be present without the others, as the research and insights from these thought leaders demonstrates.

Amy Edmonson on psychological safety

Professor Amy Edmonson is the Novartis Professor of Leadership at Harvard Business School and author of *The Fearless Organization* (2019). She defines psychological safety as 'a climate in which people are comfortable expressing and being themselves' (p.xvi).

Her research demonstrates that in the presence of psychological safety, we are more likely to take the interpersonal risk necessary to be vulnerable, and this is the mitigating factor in high-performing teams. Where interpersonal risk is high, the risk of being admonished or blamed for a mistake or missed opportunity causes people to withhold crucial information. This not only stifles creativity and learning but creates internal politics. Conversely, where interpersonal risk is low – where it is safe to learn from mistakes or offer a dissenting view – people will openly share their thoughts and ideas which are crucial components of innovation, adaptation and change.

Professor Edmondson discovered this by accident in her research into medical teams. Contrary to her expectations, she found that high-performing teams reported more mistakes (such as errors on dosages or patient care procedures) than low-performing teams. Upon further investigation, she understood that high-performing teams did not actually *make* more mistakes than low-performing teams. The difference came down to the fact that high-performing teams felt safe to report mistakes so that everyone had the opportunity to learn from them. In high-performing teams, the risk to relationships (or 'interpersonal risk') was low because team members put the wellbeing of patients ahead of their own needs.

In other words, they were able to put niceties aside and see feedback as an opportunity to improve the experience of their patients, and not a threat to their reputation or standing in the team. In Edmonson's research, psychological safety was the mitigating factor in performance – mistakes were seen as learning opportunities and not reasons to admonish, shame or blame.

Brené Brown on vulnerability

Brené Brown is a Research Professor at the University of Houston, and world leading expert on vulnerability. In her 2018 book *Dare to Lead*, she defines vulnerability as 'the emotion that we experience during times of uncertainty, risk and emotional exposure' (p.23). When we feel challenging emotions like frustration, confusion, anger, fear, sadness or shame – we feel vulnerable. These emotions are real, regardless of how experienced, competent or 'strong' we are. No matter how many times I've stepped on a stage to deliver a talk, my heart races every single time! These emotions are there specifically because I care about my performance and want the audience to take something worthwhile from the experience.

How often are you experiencing uncertainty, risk and emotional exposure? My guess is, often, if not always. Vulnerability is a common emotion when leading in business. Certainty is what we seek but every business decision carries an element of risk.

This is bad news for leaders who believe that vulnerability is weakness, or that they must never show uncertainty in the boardroom or any room. Brown's research suggests that the opposite is true – vulnerability is not a weakness. In fact, she says there can be no courage without vulnerability. She commonly asks this question of her audiences: 'Can you give me a single example of courage that you've witnessed in your own life that did not require experiencing vulnerability?' (p.23). To be brave and to have courage is to acknowledge vulnerability and to lean in anyway. There is no strength without vulnerability.

> **To be brave and to have courage is to acknowledge vulnerability and to lean in anyway. There is no strength without vulnerability.**

Brown dispels the myth that trust comes before vulnerability. She argues they come hand in hand: 'We need to trust to be vulnerable, and we need to be vulnerable to trust,' (p.30) she says. To build trust, one must first be vulnerable and extend the hand of trust. Trust is built iteratively, over many small acts of courage where people reveal their true selves to one another and build on those experiences until the bonds become so strong, that trust is a given.

Simon Sinek on trusting teams

Simon Sinek is a *New York Times* bestselling author and inspirational speaker on leadership. His TED Talk 'Start with Why' has over 11 million views, and his book by the same name has been on bestseller lists for years. He helped organisations understand the power of purpose in driving both team and consumer behaviour. While Sinek emphasises purpose as a powerful motivator, he similarly emphasises the importance of trust as a foundation stone for high-performing teams. Sinek defines trusting teams as teams made up of people who feel safe around each other. They feel safe to express their feelings, ask for help, admit mistakes and work through problems. He says: 'When we work on a Trusting Team, we feel safe to express vulnerability.'

In a trusting team, we feel safe to point out the flaws in our process, the gaps in our vision, the ways we are working that don't sustain us. We feel we can have feedback conversations, because we trust that the group will go with us on the journey and be willing to share account-ability instead of denying the existence of a problem or blaming any single individual.

Teams with low trust will only ever suggest 'safe' options. These are ideas and options with low-to-moderate risks, but which also have low-to-moderate upsides. Teams who make it safe to share feelings of uncertainty are more likely to surface issues, apply more considered thinking, and ultimately make better decisions that more members can buy into.

Paradoxically, overfocusing on results can lead to low performance, as was the case with the CEO of the global software engineering firm described earlier. This breeds a 'succeed at all costs' mentality where the work is treated as more important than people. To be high performing, teams must deprioritise performance and prioritise trust building. Only then can they create the conditions that allow them to leverage their shared pool of intelligence. In his 2019 bestselling book *The Infinite Game* Sinek says: 'When leaders are willing to prioritise trust over performance, performance almost always follows. However, when leaders have laser focus on performance above all else, the culture inevitably suffers.' (p.130).

THE BOND OF RESPECT

If trust is essential to vulnerability, respect is essential for team members to show up and lean in with their full complement of talents and strengths. To develop the bond of respect, is to develop a high level of openness, appreciation and acceptance of difference. This ultimately allows teams to benefit from the true advantage that diversity brings.

For decades, teams have been using personality profiling tools like the Myers-Briggs Type Indicator (MBTI) or the DiSC personality test in team-building workshops. While these tools are great for building self-awareness, the main way they support team building is by demonstrating the value of difference. By understanding one's own personality type and the relative strengths and weaknesses associated with that type, we may come to appreciate how other's strengths complement our own. A robust team is not one where everyone interprets the world in the same way, but one in which members think and act in divergent ways.

> **A robust team is not one where everyone interprets the world in the same way, but one in which members think and act in divergent ways.**

Of course, diversity comes not just from differences in personality, but also from differences in ethnicity, gender, sexual orientation, religion and ability. The business case for Diversity, Equity and Inclusion (DEI) is well-documented in research by McKinsey and Company cited in their *Why Diversity Matters* online article (2015). This study examined the composition of top management and boards in 366 public companies across a range of industries in Canada, Latin America, the UK and the US. They found that racially and ethnically diverse companies are 35% more likely to perform better, and that companies with gender diversity are 15% more likely to outperform competitors.

In Australia, while we acknowledge the advantage that diversity brings to workplaces, we are slow to act. Research by the Australian HR Institute (AHRI) undertaken in late 2022 reveals there is a gap between employer awareness, intent and action. While most HR professionals (84%) see DEI as critical to the future success of their organisation, only half (50%) agree that their organisation is putting enough focus on DEI (p. 3).

So why don't we embrace diversity quicker? Why must we set diversity targets in organisations to push ourselves to create more diverse teams?

The answer is that while diversity can be a significant competitive advantage it can also be a source of conflict. It is a natural human tendency to gravitate towards people who are 'like us' – people who will validate perspectives and our points of view, rather than pick out the holes and flaws in our thinking. Difference makes us uncomfortable, but if we can contain our own discomfort and see beyond our own egos to the advantages that difference brings, it can also be the fastest track to innovation and growth.

Canva is an Australian success story[1] and an example of a company actively embracing diversity and inclusion as a driver of growth. While they acknowledge they still have a way to go, Canva actively set and are accountable to diversity metrics in their teams. As reported on their website in 2021,[2] 50% of roles hired in the US were women, 21% of engineering hires in Australia were women (compared to the Australian 19% average), and 41% of product hires were women (compared to the Australian 37% average). Canva Co-Founder and COO Cliff Obrecht believes that 'a diverse team is critical to enabling differences in thinking' and that 'diversity in thought and creativity enables better decision making and is a benchmark for success' (quoted on their website). Canva is available in over 190 countries and has been translated to over 100 languages, an achievement made possible by the breadth and diversity of the Canva team.

The Canva founders themselves are an example of diversity. Melanie Perkins was born in Perth, Western Australia to an Australian-born teacher and a Malaysian engineer of Filipino and Sri Lankan descent. Her partner Cliff Obrecht was also born in Perth WA. As the CEO and COO respectively, the two are now listed as one of the top 10 wealthiest couple on the Australian Financial Review Rich List in 2024. While having a diverse leadership team from the very beginning does not necessarily guarantee success, it does set the tone for hiring decisions and inclusion practices that determine the company culture.

When it comes to building respect in teams, it's important to remember that we don't need to *like* someone to *respect* them. We don't need to be friends with our colleagues, we may never choose to hang out with them outside work. But this does not mean that we cannot develop a healthy level of respect. Friendship, even love, can emerge from a relationship built on respect. But neither are a prerequisite for respect.

---

1   In February 2024, investors and employees were selling shares in a secondary transaction at a valuation of US$26 billion. This makes it one of the largest secondary transactions in the industry's history. Reported on LinkedIn by Bilal Noorgat CA CFA.

2   https://www.canva.com/newsroom/news/The-importance-of-diversity-at-Canva/

Teams who foster mutual respect contain a high level of regard for one another's strengths and talents – a deep appreciation for the value that each member brings to the collective. Instead of seeing difference as a threat to one's own ego, to respect someone is to hold them in 'unconditional positive regard', a concept introduced by Carl Rogers and the humanistic psychologists in the 1970s. That is, to hold someone in high esteem regardless of one's own preferences and judgements towards them.

> **Teams who foster mutual respect contain a high level of regard for one another's strengths and talents – a deep appreciation for the value that each member brings to the collective.**

To show respect is to accept others for their quirks, differences and nuances of behaviour – to seek out their virtues and values – and appreciate the ways they challenge your thinking instead of feeling threatened by them. On the flipside, when we feel respected, we are more likely to show up, to reveal our strengths and talents, to share our views openly and not shy away from the debate for fear of judgement or retribution.

In connected teams, all members understand each other's roles and the strengths they bring. They take time to understand the depth and breadth of knowledge and experiences available to them – and they celebrate the opportunity of diversity instead of feeling threatened by it. I always ask my leaders two questions: How can you build a team with the most diverse thinking possible? And secondly: How can you help that team lean into their differences and appreciate diversity?

In summary, connected teams form strong bonds based on mutual trust and mutual respect, allowing them to tap into their experiences as valid sources of information that lead to more innovative, holistic and sustainable solutions that benefit the business and the communities they serve.

13

The moments that break

Trust and respect are hard won and easily broken. There are common traps that keep us stuck in dysfunction junction. Falling into these traps is frustrating. They make team interactions painful, boring and predictable. Learning how to recognise and avoid these traps is key to leadership. If you want to build a team of people who enjoy being together and do their best work together, then you need to avoid the moments that break.

THE SOLUTION TRAP – STARTING WITH THE WRONG PROBLEM IN MIND

When teams fall into the solution trap, they jump into solution-finding without first attempting to understand the problem they are solving. For example, a leadership team may come together to make a 'quick decision' on the key priorities to plug a revenue gap in the following quarter's forecasted earnings, a fairly common scenario in private enterprise. They throw out ideas to increase sales. The sales director rebuffs most ideas and asserts their first idea as the best one. An action plan is devised.

Not only does this approach not lead to the best solution, it starts at the wrong place. What if the problem is not with sales? What if the problem is in the quality of the product? Or the customer segment they are targeting? Or in the capabilities of their team? What if the problem is in how they are leading and communicating expectations and priorities?

The solution trap diminishes the opportunity to tap into collective capacity, because it prevents the members of the group from drawing on the richness of their lived experiences in relation to the real issue at hand.

Effective decision-making involves three key steps: problem identification, solution creation, and decision generation.

Joy Paul Guilford was an American psychologist who introduced us to the concepts of convergent and divergent thinking in the 1950s. It looks something like this:

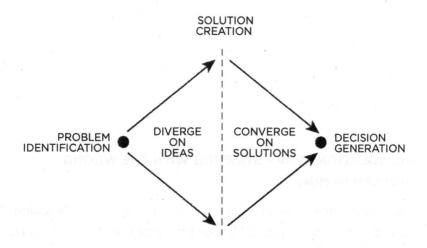

- **Step 1: Problem identification.** Agree on the problem we are solving before we start working on solutions.

- **Step 2: Diverge on ideas.** Don't just stop on the first or second option. Invite input on the full scope of options available to the team. Push the thinking beyond the immediate obvious answer, and beyond what the 'expert' thinks.

- **Step 3: Converge on solutions.** Boil down the best ideas. Divergent and convergent thinking are the ways we create solutions.

- **Step 4: Decision generation.** Agree on the criteria for the decision, and choose the best option that meets the criteria. For example – you may choose the fastest option, or the option that yields the best result for the customer, or the cheapest option, or the option with the least risk attached to it.

If we start with the wrong problem in mind, the whole process is moot. First stopping to agree on what problem we are solving ensures that the decision-making effort will yield the best outcomes possible for the team and the business.

THE DEBATE TRAP – LOCKED IN DEBATE WITH A WINNER AND A LOSER

When teams come together to solve problems or make decisions, it's very easy to get locked into a debate where there are two sides to an argument and only one wins. It starts out like this. The team gets together for a meeting. The boss pitches an idea they had overnight about how to solve a problem. The operations manager provides her viewpoint. The sales manager quickly rebuffs with: 'I disagree. I think we should do this.' The operations manager steps back in to justify her initial idea. Before we know it the two are hashing it out and everyone else is listening, figuring out which side they agree with more. Each individual's own view and opinion is now coloured by the debate unfolding.

Debates turn discussions into tennis matches – with two protagonists fighting it out to win a point, and everyone else acting as spectators, deciding which winner to back. We think that through debate, the better idea wins. But sometimes, it's not the better idea that wins – it's the person who is more skilled at communicating, voicing their idea, or with the most positional authority to whom others are more likely to defer. But what about the third side? Or the fourth side? Problems are often multidimensional – especially wicked problems that require systems thinking. What can happen with debates is that we feel we must win the argument to validate the idea. But the truth is, all ideas or opinions have merit – they do not need to be proven correct or worthy to be considered as part of the discussion.

A leadership team I have worked with for many years often falls into this trap. I am their appointed facilitator, and even I fall into this trap – it is very seductive! We were debating how to best define a particular aspect of their strategy – whether we wanted to call it 'happy people' or 'successful people'. It went back and forth for 20 minutes. Then another member of the team suggested a third option – how about 'thriving people'. Instantly we all agreed this new idea was better. When we are locked in debate, the simplest way out is to leverage collective capacity and open the sphere of ideas.

For a comprehensive set of methods for doing better thinking and avoiding the debate trap, visit Chapter 9.

THE SAVIOUR TRAP – THINKING THAT THE BOSS HAS ALL THE ANSWERS

The most common challenge that a CEO (or any team boss) faces is shutting down the creative spark whenever they walk in the room. Suddenly, everyone who was previously chatty waits to hear what the boss has to say before contributing.

There are two main reasons for this:

1. The boss has the most positional power in the room. No-one wants to say or do something 'stupid' in front of the key decision-maker who has the power to make or break careers.

2. There is a perception that because they are the most senior, they are also the most experienced or talented in the room. This is not always the case. The boss may be a great people leader, or a subject matter expert in a particular domain, but this does not make them the authority on every challenge in business.

The paradox of being the boss is that your job is to bring talented people into the business and encourage them to share their useful ideas, and yet your very presence can stifle that objective.

For this reason, a CEO I work with insists on being the last to speak whenever the team are brainstorming or sharing their viewpoints, because his opinion colours the sharing of everyone else in the room.

Another CEO I work with only joins the 'top' and 'tail' of strategic planning workshops – the morning of the first day and the afternoon of the last day – again purely to encourage everyone to own the space and share their ideas unfiltered. He sets the scene with his vision, leaves the team to come up with the big-picture plans and ideas – and then comes back to hear their views and give them feedback.

Timothy Clark is an Oxford University–trained social scientist and founder of LeaderFactor. In his 2020 book *The 4 Stages of Psychological Safety* he recommends more ways CEOs and team leaders can avoid the saviour trap:

- Assign someone else to chair the meeting – share power.

- Don't sit at the head of the table – make yourself accessible.

- Create warmth and informality – create a relaxed vibe.

- Stimulate thinking and inquiry with statements like 'I don't know…', 'help me think this through…' and 'I wonder why…' – put your opinion on a level playing field.

- Encourage those who challenge your thinking with statements like 'I'm keen to understand your perspective…' – make it safe for a diversity of views.

In modern times where problems are complex and markets are volatile, there are no precedents. The boss does not have all the answers, they are just more willing to take the risk and lead teams to innovate new solutions to organisational challenges.

THE BLAME TRAP – THINKING IT'S NOT MY FAULT, IT'S YOURS

When teams get caught up in the blame trap, they are inventing an 'us vs them' scenario that enables them to abdicate responsibility and avoid dealing with the problem. The blame trap creates a false sense of security. 'I've done my part – it's someone else's fault things have gone wrong' is not the mindset of team players or people thinking systemically. Doing your part is important, but what is also important is how all the parts fit together to create a whole. You are not responsible just for your piece of the puzzle, but how your piece fits to create a picture.

Poor performance in organisations rarely has a single cause. There are of course the 'bad eggs' – individuals who cannot or will not behave in accordance with the ethics, standards and values of the team or organisation they serve. These individuals must be given feedback, and either helped to meet expectations or moved on. However, in my experience, 'bad eggs' are the exception rather than the rule to underperformance. For performance in an organisation to lift, we must first look at the cohesion and performance of the executive or leadership team. They set the tone for performance through how they take individual and collective accountability for results.

> **Poor performance in organisations rarely has a single cause.**

Leadership teams fall into the blame trap when they look for reasons for poor performance outside of themselves such as:

- supply chain issues
- the economy
- the competition
- underperforming employees
- the board
- the suppliers.

They also fall into this trap when they blame each other for poor performance. Instead of sharing responsibility, they blame the:

- Head of Sales for poor sales
- Head of Operations for delays in supply, production or logistics
- Head of People for lack of access to key skills and capabilities
- Head of Marketing for brand reputation
- Head of Finance for poor margins
- Head of Technology for inefficient systems and processes.

All these problems do indeed have an external locus of control (there are elements that are outside of their control). But leaders are better together when they look inward and understand what they can take accountability for – where they have an internal locus of control.

The blame trap diminishes collective capacity because the group are giving over their power to the 'other' instead of accepting their own responsibility as part of a system and working through how they can influence the outcome through their own actions.

Instead of playing the blame game, play the accountability game. Assume responsibility for the part you play and instead of attributing blame, seek solutions.

14

Leverage collective capacity

'The test of a first-rate intelligence is the ability to hold two opposed ideas in mind at the same time and still retain the ability to function.'

Scott Fitzgerald

THE SIMPLE MATH OF COLLECTIVE CAPACITY

To tap into collective capacity is to tap into the full range of resources available to any team or group that forms to perform a task or function. These include mental, emotional, physical and spiritual resources (like our values and beliefs). Tapping into collective capacity gives teams access to exponential resources.

To tap into collective capacity is to first decide to work as a team, instead of a group. Back in Chapter 1, we explored the difference between a team versus a group. A group operates in independent ways, while a team operates in interdependent ways.

Think about it as a simple maths equation.

When a team the size of, for example, seven members operate as a group, there are only six relationship dynamics to draw on: each individual's relationship with the team's leader. But when a group of seven operate as a team, there are 7×7 relationships, or 49 relationships to draw on. That's a powerful increase in relationship dynamics – and with that comes exponential thinking. This is demonstrated in the figure below.

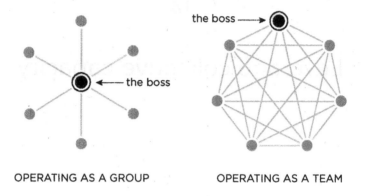

OPERATING AS A GROUP   OPERATING AS A TEAM

When the 'boss' of the team relates as *one of* the team (as an individual with ultimate decision-making power, yes; but with no more or less intelligence, agency or uniqueness than any other individual in the team), the collective capacity of the whole is enhanced beyond a limited number of relationships.

When a team of experienced professionals makes space for rigorous intellectual curiosity, the group transforms into a team. They innovate, loop each other in, build on each other's ideas, challenge openly and enhance their decision-making in ways that any single individual could not do on their own. As Scott Fitzgerald's quote suggests – they can hold two seemingly opposed ideas in mind and still function.

When a team of experienced professionals makes space for rigorous intellectual curiosity, the group transforms into a team.

The more diverse the viewpoints, the greater the opportunity for innovation. Frans Johansson is an entrepreneur and author of *The Medici Effect* (2017). He defines the Medici Effect as a phenomenon that occurs when diverse fields, cultures and disciplines intersect and become the catalyst for innovation and creative breakthroughs. He draws its name from the influential Medici family of 14th-century Florence. The Medicis were known for their patronage of the arts and their ability to bring together thinkers, artists, scientists and merchants from various backgrounds – a cohesive force that ultimately led to the Renaissance. In a similar vein, the Medici Effect suggests that when people with different perspectives, knowledge and experiences come together, this creates a fertile ground for new ideas and solutions.

WHEN SIZE DOES MATTER

When it comes to teams, size does matter.

As companies grow, one of the most important decisions they will make is determining when teams get too big, how to structure and restructure, and when to create layers of leadership.

A scale-up I worked with reached a point at which it needed to undertake an organisational restructure. There were multiple reasons for this change, but one of the main pain points driving the change was that the CEO simply had too many direct reports and this was creating bottlenecks in decision-making. With increasing pressures on his time dealing with regulatory challenges, mergers and acquisitions, he simply could not give his direct reports the time they needed to progress decisions quickly enough. The leadership team overall needed fewer members, with more decision-making authority, to effectively perform their duties as a leadership function and execute on strategic plans and priorities.

So what size is the right size?

Bob Sutton is a bestselling author, Stanford Professor and organisational psychologist. He believes that 'four to six members is the best team size for most tasks, that no work team should have more than 10 members, and that performance problems and interpersonal friction increases exponentially as team size increases'.[1]

---

1   https://www.linkedin.com/pulse/20140303152358-15893932-why-big-teams-suck/

In the early days of Amazon, Jeff Bezos instilled the 'two pizza rule', where every internal team should be small enough that it can be fed with two pizzas[1]. While this simple concept hasn't been applied as a blanket rule, it does seem to be true for the team at the top with only seven executive officers at the helm of the multi-billion dollar company. That's enough for at least two large slices per person[2]!

What about in leadership teams? The leadership team needs to be big enough to bring a diversity of perspectives and skills, but small enough to allow for efficient decision-making and effective communication.

A study by Bain and Company found where there are seven people in a decision-making group, personal and team performance is highest. After seven people, each extra member reduces decision effectiveness by 10%[3].

How about another kind of leadership team as mentioned back in Chapter 3 – the board? The Australian Institute for Company Directors (AICD) is the largest director membership organisation in the world, providing education and advocating on director issues on behalf of members. A 2022 AICD report noted that board size has received attention in US governance literature because of its correlation between large board sizes (15 to 20 members) and poor performance of the company. 'The larger the board, the greater potential for creating factions, as well as risking disharmony and difficulty in effective decision making' (p. 41).

The AICD avoid prescriptions for board size, but rather provide 'rules of thumb' according to company and industry type. For example, they recommend board sizes of eight to 12 for large ASX-listed companies; six to eight for medium ASX-listed companies; four to six for small ASX-listed companies; and one to four for proprietary companies[4].

---

1   https://www.theguardian.com/technology/2018/apr/24/the-two-pizza-rule-and-the-secret-of-amazons-success?CMP=share_btn_url

2   https://ir.aboutamazon.com/officers-and-directors/default.aspx

3   https://www.bain.com/insights/effective-decision-making-and-the-rule-of-7

4   https://www.aicd.com.au/content/dam/aicd/pdf/tools-resources/director-tools/board/board-size-director-tool.pdf

When it comes to team size, the research suggests that bigger is not necessarily better. There is a tipping point where size becomes dysfunctional to the overall performance of the group. It seems that the magic number of seven plus or minus two applies here.

When it comes to leadership teams, whether it's on the smaller or larger end of that range depends on the stage and complexity of the company.

In the start-up phase, a smaller leadership team may be more appropriate. Smaller teams tend to be more agile and, with fewer people involved, able to make decisions more quickly. In smaller teams, each person is more likely to have a deep understanding of the company's goals and strategy. They are also more likely to have a stronger sense of camaraderie and shared purpose, which can lead to better collaboration.

As the company grows, more functions need to be added and leadership teams often grow in size. Larger leadership teams can benefit from a more diverse range of skills and perspectives. A larger team may be better equipped to handle complex challenges and be more effective at managing a larger number of employees.

Where leadership teams start to exceed the magic number of seven plus or minus two, it is wise to instil leadership layers – an extended leadership team reporting to the executive leadership team – who are empowered to parcel out the programs of work and compartmentalise projects into tangible actions within sub-groups and individuals.

The decision about the best size for the leadership team depends on the needs of the company, the stage of its growth, and the skills of the people involved. Ultimately, the focus should always be on selecting the right people with the right skills and experience, who together offer the collective capacity necessary for driving the organisation forward.

The decision about the best size for the leadership team depends on the needs of the company, the stage of its growth, and the skills of the people involved.

Back to the scale-up I worked with. Once the CEO had made the decision to restructure, he reduced his direct reports from 13 to six. Meetings were far more productive, and the strength of connection, trust and openness within the leadership team instantly improved. Decisions were made with far more conviction, and their camaraderie was stronger as a result. Once the change was made, my client wondered why he'd waited for so long! He had been concerned about disengaging the other seven members of the group, but in fact the reverse happened – they each finally had the level of focus and attention they needed from a boss who had the time to listen, and were each more empowered to take action on their programs of work.

WHERE CEOS LEARN TO LEAN-IN TO VULNERABILITY

Leveraging collective capacity is a skillset that can be learned and applied. It does not rely on time spent together. It relies on groups of people coming together, working as a team, agreeing on specific principles for engagement, and on bringing oneself to the process with humility, courage and grace. It does not require any previous experience leading, but it does require that the members of the group be generous with their sharing and genuine with their listening. That they speak from lived experience, share their feelings, and withhold judgement.

> **Leveraging collective capacity is a skillset that can be learned and applied.**

One place where business leaders learn to be better together is Young Presidents Organization – or YPO.

YPO is a global leadership community of chief executives, with the purpose of *Building Better Leaders through learning and idea exchange*. YPO is a membership organisation, run by members, for members. Members are under 45 years of age and lead organisations that meet specific size criteria. Entrepreneurs' Organization (EO) is very similar – with the only exception being that it is directed at founders and entrepreneurs and therefore has different minimum entry criteria. These entry criteria ensure that members share similar challenges that come with being an organisational leader.

Leadership can be lonely. By joining YPO or EO (depending on the stage of business growth), members are no longer alone as they meet and connect with other leaders who share their unique view from the top, with all the benefits and challenges that leadership of companies brings.

Both YPO and EO are organised into regions and chapters. Membership opens the doors to networks of leaders in one's own region, and indeed industry. But far and away the greatest espoused benefit for members is access to a Forum. A Forum is a group of eight to 10 members from non-competitive industries who meet monthly in an atmosphere of complete confidentiality and trust, and who follow a very specific set of meeting protocols and processes to maximise the learning, sharing and growth for all members.

The 'power of Forum' is regularly discussed in YPO and EO circles. It is powerful because what members learn when they join a Forum are the principles and practices that enable relative strangers to form bonds of confidentiality, trust, respect and authentic connection very quickly.

The process of Forum is a language that allows members to cut directly to the heart of human experience, to tap into collective capacity with minimal face time or shared experience.

In Forum, members are actively tapping into the well of human experience and they are leveraging shared capability in the service of learning how to be better leaders, and better people.

The first time I experienced the power of Forum directly was when I trained as a YPO Certified Forum Facilitator. For four days, I sat in a circle of chairs with 10 other professional facilitators in a hotel in Narita, Japan, to practice and perfect the structured processes and protocols of a Forum meeting. The meeting requires equal commitment and full engagement from all members for the value of the experience to be realised.

In one particularly powerful moment, I shared a story that triggered deep shame so acute it brought on tears that I couldn't control. I was surprised by the tears – I hadn't realised I was still carrying guilt, resentment, even fear over this event. But here it was coming out in the most vulnerable way possible. The story I shared was of a moment of failure I experienced with a client who was disappointed with the way I facilitated a workshop for them. Members of their group complained that I hadn't met the brief. It blindsided me – as I hadn't picked up their dissatisfaction on the day. This news came as a surprise and the fact that I'd missed it was what shook me more than the feedback itself.

My fellow facilitators sitting in the circle with me listened to my story. They did not attempt to console, pacify or counsel me. Instead, they each stepped in with their own experiences of shame of failure, or how the fear of failure was holding them back. One by one, they spoke from their own experience – both of what had happened to them and how those events had made them feel.

In listening to their stories, I felt something shift. The empathy I was feeling towards their stories, I realised could and should also be directed towards myself. People make mistakes. Mistakes are a natural part of learning. If they were worthy of forgiveness, then so was I. In that moment, I began to grasp emotionally, as much as rationally, that failure is sometimes a necessary and difficult part of growth.

Inherent in the design of a Forum meeting is the necessity to be vulnerable. To share not just issues, challenges and opportunities, but the reasons why these things are important, and how they make us feel. This sharing is made possible by a number of key principles of Forum success. These are:

1. Confidentiality – an absolute bond of trust that nothing shall be shared outside the meeting, to no-one, and never.

2. Commitment – a commitment to turning up on time, every time, and remaining fully present.

3. Protocol – no 'advice giving', only 'experience sharing'.

4. Meeting structure – a clear structured meeting process with strict time limits to maximise sharing and learning for all group members.

5. Leadership – from a peer-nominated moderator who chairs the meeting and maintains the protocols.

6. Membership – a group size of eight to 10 is maintained as this maximises perspectives shared within the given time limits.

7. Shared vision, mission, values – a clear agreed reason for meeting and connecting.

8. Renewal – a commitment to going on retreat and evaluating the health of the Forum annually.

While the purpose of Forum is not the same as the purpose of a leadership team or any other work team, the principles and practices learned can be applied across contexts.

The skills that members learn in Forum are directly transferable to how leaders lead within their organisations, families and communities. They learn very quickly that to get the best out of others, to create safety and allow for creativity and innovation to flourish, they must lead differently. Leadership is not about 'bossing', telling, directing, forcing, or controlling in any way. That is an old, outdated doctrine established in a different era. Instead, they learn that leadership is about creating environments where experiences can be shared 'unfiltered', where access to the collective wisdom creates opportunity for new ideas and new learning to occur, and where vulnerability is a strength, not a weakness.

What the YPO and Forum experience has taught me is that to leverage collective capacity is to learn a set of protocols that allow us to gain access to the power of human experience.

When these conditions are present, the collective capacity of human experience becomes a bottomless source of knowledge, that, when combined with expert data analysis supplied by the likes of AI, informs better decision-making.

15

The dynamics of a team

If the goal is to build on a more healthy, high-functioning team dynamic, then we must understand the protocols that build trust and respect. We must understand the mechanics of how teams behave in an effort to be more cohesive and find team synergy.

A team dynamic is the result of a series of interactions. It is the net result of how one person influences another, and vice versa, multiplied by the number of people in a team.

To understand whether the dynamic is healthy or unhealthy – constructive or dysfunctional – we must break-down their interactions to component behaviours. We must look at the units of interaction that determine whether a team will be better together, or better off alone.

When teams interact, there are five basic observable functions that determine the nature of the dynamic that emerges between them. These are the five key interactions of a team, described in the table overleaf.

This table provides a simple tool to diagnose group dynamics and a language for teams to discuss ways to foster greater team synergy.

The five key interactions of a team are:

Contribution	The proportion of individual contribution to the group
Voice	The honesty and diversity of views shared
Listening	The degree to which ideas are understood and incorporated
Questioning	The degree of curiosity, inquiry, and testing of ideas
Decision-making	The process for how decisions are ultimately made

CONTRIBUTION

To work as a team, it is important that all members contribute their ideas and perspective. The dynamic of the team is influenced by the proportion of individual contribution by each member of the group. Every team member's input is valuable, and a diverse range of perspectives fuels productive discussions. It's important for individuals to contribute their insights, ideas, thoughts and feelings, but also be mindful of not dominating the conversation.

Dominant voices take up space and rarely make room for others to step in. Sometimes they are those with the greatest positional authority – they assume more airtime because they have more power. Other times, it's just the extroverts whose signature trait is doing their thinking *as they speak*, who, in their enthusiasm, forget to create a gap in contributions to allow for the introverts who are waiting patiently to step in.

Allowing space for all voices to be shared encourages a more inclusive environment and ensures the group does not miss out on any gems of wisdom that might otherwise be withheld due to lack of opportunity to voice them.

VOICE

Just allowing space for all voices to be shared does not necessarily guarantee honesty. If contribution is about opening the door, voice is about stepping into the room.

Voice is about speaking your truth, sharing your views and empowering yourself to stand in your own conviction.

To have a voice, you must first listen to it. What is your voice? What are your views? What are you trying to say? How does your view differ from others and how is it the same? To find your voice – skip back to Part II.

Idea repeating is just white noise. There is nothing more frustrating than being in a meeting where people repeat one another's ideas as ways of validating what is being said. If you have nothing new to add, say: 'Echo!' If you have a variation to add, then say: 'I agree, *and* I add this…'. Or if you have a different idea, then say so. Where there is trust and respect in a group, your controversial idea, dissenting voice, or contrary view will add to the breadth and depth of ideas that the group may work with. So long as you are not being contrary in an effort to gain control, speak up and share your voice. Start by saying: 'I have a different perspective to share.'

When trust is absent, where there is no psychological safety, voice will be masked or muted. Individuals will present safe ideas and withhold their vulnerabilities. When there is trust and safety, individuals will share honest and authentic views, bringing the rich variety of perspectives that are the fuel for innovation and change.

> **When trust is absent, where there is no psychological safety, voice will be masked or muted.**

LISTENING

There is no point creating space for authentic voice to be shared if there is no place for it to land. Sharing voice is important, but listening to others' voices is equally important. When we are actively listening, we are creating space for understanding.

We all know the difference between being heard and being understood. We all know that active listening is not just waiting for one's turn to speak but allowing others' ideas to settle in our own consciousness before responding.

Dr Steven Covey is the acclaimed author of *The Seven Habits of Highly Effective People* (1989). One such habit is to 'seek first to understand, then to be understood'. By seeking to understand, we experience empathy. If we are only waiting our own turn to speak, we are blocking our opportunity for empathy.

Through empathy, we improve openness to differences. We open our minds to multiple viewpoints that may at first seem in conflict with one another, but that nonetheless broaden the scope of what can be worked with. We can hear different voices and allow one voice to be influenced by others.

It is a very brave team who can go wide and deep on the problems, challenges and opportunities that fall within their scope to address. When we truly listen and seek to understand others, we set up the conditions for mutual trust and respect. We foster learning and growth. This can only happen where we go beyond turn taking, and actively listen to the heart of the messages being conveyed.

> **When we truly listen and seek to understand others, we set up the conditions for mutual trust and respect.**

QUESTIONING

It is only through questioning where the 'leverage' in 'leverage collective capacity' happens. Questioning allows teams to invite, stack and build upon ideas – to challenge assumptions and identify gaps in knowledge.

> **Questioning allows teams to invite, stack and build upon ideas – to challenge assumptions and identify gaps in knowledge.**

As we learned back in Chapter 2, team synergy is achieved when together, we're better. That is, when the group finds a better solution together than any one individual could do alone.

Contribution is necessary for adding 'data' into the room. Voice is necessary to ensure that data is authentic, real and diverse. Listening is necessary to maintain a safe and respectful place where diversity can be accepted. Questioning is necessary to expand the range of options available, explore their merits and allow the most reasonable option to emerge.

There are different types of questions, each having a different impact on interaction dynamic. There are:

- **Closed questions:** End in a one-word answer. They are useful for checking understanding, but minimise interaction and are therefore limited in building trust. They often start with when, where, are, do, did, could or should.

- **Open questions:** Invite more than a one-word answer. They invite contribution and voice. They activate listening. Open questions often start with what, which, how and why.

- **Leading questions:** Guide or encourage others towards an intended answer. They are used by lawyers when 'leading the witness'. Leading questions are useful in marketing or sales, but less useful in keeping lines of inquiry open. An example is: 'Would you like blue or red? Which shade of blue…navy blue or sky blue?'

- **Exploratory questions:** Enable us to go deeper on a particular line of inquiry. They help us gain a more complete picture or richer understanding. An example is: 'Tell me more about why you like the colour blue? How does the colour blue make you feel?'

To question is to adopt a coaching style. To ask versus tell. When you explore through questions, often the solutions reveal themselves, reducing the need for conflict or debate.

DECISION-MAKING

How teams work together to make decisions is a key indicator of their team dynamic. Teams can either make decisions based on conformity, compromise, or consensus.

> **How teams work together to make decisions is a key indicator of their team dynamic.**

Conformity is when members *hide* or mask their true thoughts and feelings. It is driven by a desire to avoid blame and tends to lead to *sub-standard* solutions that maintain the status quo. In this scenario, the team's performance is only going to be as good as the most powerful member.

This is how decisions by conformity typically roll:

1. Ideas are thrown around.
2. The HiPPO wins (highest paid person's opinion)!

However (as previously mentioned back in Chapter 8) the HiPPO is not necessarily the one with the most knowledge or capability in dealing with the issue at hand; hence sub-standard performance and lacklustre engagement prevail.

Compromise occurs when members *concede* to one another. It is driven by a desire to avoid conflict, and tends to lead to *average* solutions, because the group are seeking a safe middle ground that everyone can at least live with. The 'happy middle ground' might be a happy place for the team, but it's rarely the superior outcome for the business or organisation. When groups use voting as a tool for decision-making, they are compromising by going with a majority vote that represents the majority, not the collective.

Consensus is when team members seek to find agreement. It is driven by a desire to find the *best* solution for the business or organisation they serve. Juries must work this way – they must find consensus on a verdict beyond all reasonable doubt. This approach denotes a stretch – it requires team members to consider multiple angles and form evidence-based assessments. It takes extra work, but it guarantees stronger buy-in and delivers a better solution.

There is a caveat on consensus when working in business. Being clear about who you're trying to find consensus with is important. An executive team of seven to 10 members working together to find consensus is a worthwhile endeavour. A sales field team of 20 working for consensus is going to be impossible. The group size and decision-making authority will have an impact on whether consensus is achievable or even desirable. In the end, the person with the decision-making authority will make the final call but knowing where others stand on the decision will influence how it is ultimately carried out.

DIAGNOSE YOUR TEAM DYNAMIC

Is your team interacting in ways that enables the group to leverage collective capacity and achieve team synergy?

The table below summarises how each of the five team interactions are experienced depending on the dynamic of the team.

The Five Interactions of a Team

	Dysfunctional Team	Functional Team	Team in Synergy
Contribution The proportion of individual contribution to the group	Unbalanced	Equal	Proportionate
Voice The honesty and diversity of views shared	Masked	Honest	Diverse
Listening The degree to which ideas are understood and incorporated	Turn-taking	Hearing	Active
Questioning The degree of curiosity, inquiry, and testing of ideas	Leading	Open	Exploratory
Decision-making The process for how decisions are ultimately made	Conformity	Compromise	Consensus

At **worst**, are **dysfunctional teams**. These are teams are stuck in dysfunction junction, working in ways that slow or hinder performance of the group. In dysfunctional teams:

- Contribution is unbalanced – dominant voices tend to fill the space.
- Voice is masked – true opinions are hidden in order to fit in.
- There is no listening, only turn-taking.
- Questioning is for the purpose of leading to foregone conclusions.
- Decision-making is characterised by conformity to those with the most positional or perceived power.

Better, is to be a **functional team**. When a leadership team is functional, they are adequately meeting goals and expectations:

- Contribution is equal – there is conscious effort to share space and hear all voices.
- When shared, voice is honest, real and unbiased.
- Listening is about hearing one another's views and allowing one's view to be influenced by others.
- Questioning is open, inviting discussion and debate to tease out variables.
- Decision-making is characterised by compromise – members have an equal vote, decisions are often made by majority rule.

Best, is to be a **team in synergy**. These teams are actively leveraging collective potential to perform better together than any single individual could do on their own. In teams with synergy:

- Contribution is proportionate – it's afforded to the individuals who have the most knowledge, experience or responsibility to contribute, depending on the nature of the problem to be solved.
- Voice is diverse – there is diversity of thinking and an acceptance that increasing breadth and depth of ideas contributes to better solutions.

- Listening is active – individuals do not only listen but seek to confirm their understanding by paraphrasing and checking in.

- Questioning is exploratory – expanding on good ideas and opening further possibilities for new and different pathways.

- Decision-making is characterised by consensus. Just because all individuals have power does not mean all always wield it. Decisions are driven by a desire to find the *best* solution for the business or organisation.

Where would you rate your team on each of the five functions in the above table? Are you stuck in dysfunction junction? Or are you effectively leveraging the talent and resources available to you most of the time?

The Five Interactions of a Team table has been converted into a diagnostic tool overleaf to measure to measure and score your team's dynamic.

A great way to start the conversation with your team about your dynamic is to make a copy of the page and ask everyone to complete it. Any score less than a 3 on each of the five interactions of a team represents an opportunity for improvement. Facilitate a conversation surfacing each individual's experience of the team. This will reveal any hidden tensions that exist in the way the group are working together and is a necessary step towards being able to address it. Do not be surprised if there are very different experiences of the same team. Each person's experience is valid – to lead is to create a space big enough to hold all the different experiences. This is an exercise in being vulnerable, which is a necessary part of building trust.

Working on the dynamics of a leadership team (or board, or committee or functional team) is as important as doing the work of the team. In the following chapters, we explore how to build the team dynamic towards finding team synergy.

Team Synergy Diagnostic

	Contribution	Voice	Listening	Questioning	Decision-making
	The proportion of individual contribution to the group	The honesty and diversity of views shared	The degree to which ideas are understood and incorporated	The degree of curiosity, inquiry, and testing of ideas	The process for how decisions are ultimately made
Team in Synergy Overall Score: 11-15	**Proportionate** Contribution is weighted to those with the most knowledge or experience based on the problem at hand Score: 3	**Diverse** A wide breadth and depth of ideas are actively sought and considered Score: 3	**Active** Members seek to both listen and confirm their understanding by paraphrasing and checking in Score: 3	**Exploratory** Questions expand on ideas and open further possibilities for new and different pathways Score: 3	**Consensus** Characterised by collective agreement on what will yield the best result for the business Score: 3
Functional Team Overall Score: 6-10	**Equal** There is conscious effort to share space equally and hear all voices Score: 2	**Honest** When shared, voice is honest, real, and unbiased Score: 2	**Hearing** Listening is about hearing one another's views and allowing one's view to be influenced by others. Score: 2	**Open** Questions invite discussion and debate to tease out variables on existing ideas Score: 2	**Compromise** Characterised by majority-rule, based on effective debate Score: 2
Dysfunctional Team Overall Score 0-5	**Unbalanced** Dominant voices tend to fill the space Score: 1	**Masked** True opinions are hidden in order to fit in or avoid confrontation Score: 1	**Turn-taking** There is no listening, only waiting for one's turn to speak Score: 1	**Leading** Questions lead to foregone conclusions Score: 1	**Conformity** Characterised by conformity to hierarchy, rules and procedures Score: 1
Circle	1, 2, or 3	1, 2, or 3	1, 2, or 3	1, 2, or 3	1, 2, or 3

- To think systemically is to appreciate that everything is connected.

- One of the major advantages to systems thinking is its potential to foster collaboration and cooperation. Connected teams tap into the system. Every team member's experience is a valid data point – together they provide a more complete picture.

- The second major advantage to thinking systemically is that it creates shared value. When teams adopt systems thinking they consider the impact their decisions will have on all stakeholders – including customers, suppliers, partners, investors, employees and the environment.

- Connectedness is a capability that can be developed. People strong in connectedness are adept at building communities, finding commonalities, helping others see how their efforts fit into a larger picture, and breaking down silos.

- In all relationships there are two essential ingredients that must be present for the relationship to flourish: mutual trust and mutual respect.

- Trust and respect are the bonds that tie.

- **Trust is essential to vulnerability.** Without trust, there can be no psychological safety. Trust is essential to getting at the real concerns, real viewpoints and diversity of views essential to effective problem-solving and ultimate buy-in.

- **Respect is essential to showing up.** When we show respect, we withhold judgement and seek to understand others' perspectives. We appreciate the value that diversity brings.

- Trust and respect are hard won and easily broken. There are common traps that keep us stuck in dysfunction junction.

  - **The solution trap** – where teams fall into solution-finding without first attempting to understand the problem they are solving.

- **The debate trap** – where teams become locked in debate between two opposing ideas, instead of inviting more views to open the sphere of consideration.
- **The saviour trap** – thinking that the boss has all the answers. The boss is the final decision-maker – not necessarily the person with the most knowledge or expertise.
- **The blame trap** – where teams attribute blame to forces outside of their control, instead of taking accountability and seeking solutions for the things inside their control.

- To tap into collective capacity is to tap into the full range of resources available to any team or group that forms to perform a task or function. Tapping into collective capacity gives teams access to exponential resources.

- When it comes to teams, size does matter. The research suggests there is a tipping point where size becomes dysfunctional to the overall performance of the group. The 'magic number' of seven plus or minus two applies to team size.

- Leveraging collective capacity is a skillset that can be learned and applied. YPO and EO Forums are a place where CEOs and entrepreneurs learn to tap into collective wisdom, by practicing vulnerability and openly sharing experiences.

- The five interactions of a team are the basic behavioural components that determine the dynamic of team. These are:
  - **Contribution:** The proportion of individual contribution to the group.
  - **Voice:** The honesty and diversity of views shared.
  - **Listening:** The degree to which ideas are understood and incorporated.
  - **Questioning:** The degree of curiosity, inquiry, and testing of ideas.
  - **Decision-making:** The process for how decisions are ultimately made.

- In **dysfunctional teams**, contribution is unbalanced, voice is masked, there is no listening (only turn-taking), questions are leading, and decision-making is by conformity.

- In **functional teams**, contribution is equal, voice is honest, listening is about hearing, questioning is open, and decision-making is by compromise.

- In **synergised teams**, contribution is proportionate, voice is diverse, listening is active, questioning is exploratory, and decision-making is by consensus.

- The Five Interactions of a Team table has been converted into a Team Synergy Diagnostic. Asking team members to complete the diagnostic individually, and then discussing scores collectively, gives teams insights into how they can improve their interaction dynamic.

Part IV

Be Calm

'Keep calm and carry on.'

Ministry of Information, Government of the United Kingdom, 1939

16

Keep calm and synergise

When you need help at work, who would you rather call on? The colleague who keeps a level head in a crisis or the colleague who lets stress get the better of them?

Of course, we'd all rather consult with co-workers who keep calm and carry on.

When the pressure is on, what we *don't* need is escalation and catastrophising. We need people who can bring their crucial and creative thinking capacities to the task and work through the challenge. We need people who will combine their energies in service to the problem, not get swept up into a state of stress.

Teams in synergy remain calm under pressure. When it's time to perform, they have confidence in the team knowing that together, they're better. Instead of seeing each other as adversaries in competition for more recognition or better jobs, they draw strength and inspiration from one another.

| **Teams in synergy remain calm under pressure.**

We see these teams in action all the time – surgical teams, chefs in three-hatted restaurants, orchestras in concert, jazz bands, dancers on a stage, improv groups, musicals, basketball teams, football teams in a high-stakes game, crews on film sets. What do teams in synergy in your context look like?

Make no mistake, these teams are actively choosing a calm state of mind, not having a rest. They are engaged in their work to the point of shutting everything else out. When teams keep calm and find synergy, they've entered an optimal state known as **flow**. Flow is a peak state where we both feel our best and perform our best. When we've entered flow, we're in the zone.

PEAK PERFORMANCE IS A STATE OF FLOW

Psychologist Mihaly Csikszentmihalyi (pronounced *Me-high, Chick-sent-me-high*) first coined the term 'flow' to describe a state of heightened consciousness, in which a person is fully absorbed in an activity that requires both skill and challenge.

Professor Emeritus Csikszentmihalyi was the chairperson of the University of Chicago Department of Psychology. He discovered that flow is a state of optimal experience, as 'the state in which people are so involved in an activity that nothing else seems to matter; the experience itself is so enjoyable that people will do it even at great cost, for the sheer sake of doing it.' (p.4).

Flow is the peak we are all seeking. Our best days are the ones we have flow experiences – a breakthrough, a spark of inspiration, absorption in a task so infinitely engaging that we lose track of time. Flow researchers consistently report that people experience their most creative moments in flow.

Csikszentmihalyi found that we enter flow under eight conditions:

1. **Clear goals:** It is clear what is required moment to moment – like when surfing a wave, writing code or playing a challenging piece of music.

2. **Immediate feedback:** There is constant and immediate feedback about how close you are to achieving that goal.

3. **Appropriately challenging:** Your skills match the challenge of the task. If the challenge is too high, it's stressful. But if the task isn't challenging enough, it's boring.

4. **Deep concentration:** You are free to fully concentrate on the task.

5. **Intrinsically rewarding:** The enjoyment of doing the task is its own reward.

6. **Control:** You have complete control over your own performance.

7. **Altered time:** You are so absorbed in the activity, that time feels altered – it either slows down or speeds up.

8. **Egolessness:** You lose your sense of self while in it. In fact, we often don't know we're in flow until after we've come out of it.

I like to think of flow as being at our performance edge. The place where capacity meets challenge, where performance meets potential. Our performance edge is where we are dynamically changing via the interaction with a task and the environment. We are actively learning by doing, increasing our capacity, and expanding our potential.

This state has been described as 'the most desirable state on earth' by Steven Kotler, an author, journalist and co-founder of the Flow Research Collective. Kotler uses the example of action and adventure athletes who have no choice but to be in flow to pull off death-defying feats where mistakes or hesitations have ultimate consequences. 'In flow every action, each decision, leads effortlessly, fluidly, seamlessly to the next. It's high-speed problem solving; it's being swept away by the river of ultimate performance.' (2014, p.viii)

But you don't have to be an action and adventure athlete to find flow. Researchers have discovered the most common place that people experience flow is at work, in conversations with others. Keith Sawyer, a professor of psychology and author of *Group Genius* (2007), writes that 'at work, conversation with colleagues is one of the most flow-inducing activities; managers, in particular, are most likely to be in flow when they're engaged in conversation'.

This led Sawyer to ask the question: might there be something like group flow?

SYNERGY IS GROUP FLOW

By studying jazz ensembles, Keith Sawyer discovered that improvisation groups attain a collective state of mind that he calls *group flow*. 'Group flow is a peak experience, a group performing at its top level of ability. In group flow, activity becomes spontaneous, and the group acts without thinking about it first.' (p. 33)

In fact, group flow is reported to be infinitely more enjoyable than individual flow because it is amplified by the rewarding nature of social bonding that comes with flow in a group. In studies run by Charles Walker, a psychologist from St Bonaventure University, 'solitary flow' was measured against 'coactive flow' (activities performed co-located) and 'interactive flow' (activities that involve interaction). Walker reported that the more social the activity, the higher the level of 'flow enjoyment' – the level of joy experienced in flow.

Just as there are eight conditions for solitary flow, Sawyer has reported 10 conditions for group flow. The first six are the modified 'group versions' of the individual conditions identified by Csikszentmihalyi. The other four are specific to harnessing collective genius:

1. **Clear goals:** The group goal is well understood and explicitly stated.

2. **Immediate feedback/communication:** There is constant communication about how the group is performing.

3. **Being in control:** They have complete autonomy over how the task is done.

4. **Deep concentration:** There is a clear boundary between what the group is performing and everything else.

5. **Blending egos:** Like 'egolessness' there is a 'magical moment' where everybody comes together and thinks as one mind, pre-empting one another and moving together as a unit. Keep calm and synergise.

6. **The potential for failure:** Similar to 'appropriately challenging' there is just enough risk so that it is not underwhelming, but not so much that it doesn't overwhelm.

7. **Close listening:** Everyone is fully engaged. They don't plan what they will say but instead genuinely respond to what they hear.

8. **Equal participation:** All participants play an equal role in collective co-creation.

9. **Familiarity:** They share a common language and common set of unspoken rules.

10. **Keeping it moving forward:** Always say yes. This is akin to the 'yes but' and 'yes and' thinking amplifiers we first encountered back in Chapter 9.

Teams in synergy have entered group flow. They combine their talents in creative ways to deliver exceptional outcomes, outperforming what any individual could do alone.

Synergy is a group entering the zone together. It's a place where each member is actively using their strengths and talents, collaborating, and combining their efforts in symphony with one another. Synergy is the ultimate team bonding experience. It is the Goldilocks zone – there the challenge does not overwhelm nor underwhelm collective capacity. It's just right.

| **Synergy is a group entering the zone together.**

Unlike sporting teams, dance troupes, orchestras or bands, work teams do not have the luxury of hours of training leading up to an ultimate performance. Nor do they have the opportunity to slowly build up the 10 conditions for synergy over time. Work teams, and particularly leadership teams, are expected to hit the ground running and to perform to the highest level, every day. Their training-to-performance ratio is reversed. Unlike athletes and stage performers, modern-day workers have far less training or rest times in proportion to much longer sustained periods of performance.

So how do we overcome this challenge and fast-track work teams to find group flow and work in synergy? The following chapters provide practical how-to ways for any leader to lead their team towards consistent high performance by creating the conditions for flow.

HOW TO FIND TEAM SYNERGY

Working on the dynamic of the team is as important as doing the work of the team. Teams can't achieve high performance unless they have a positive interaction dynamic.

> **Working on the dynamic of the team is as important as doing the work of the team.**

Finding team synergy is a process of turning your focus on the dynamic of the team and enabling each member to take up their roles as simultaneous leaders and followers in the group. Leadership and followership are two sides of the same coin. To lead, invites followership. To follow, empowers leaders. One does not exist without the other.

However, synergy is not a switch we can flick. We can't just turn it on and off at will. What we *can* do is create the conditions for synergy and group flow. We can considerably improve our chances for high performance by tuning into and sharpening up on the processes that lead to teamwork.

This section describes a series of exercises that you can lead to dramatically improve the nature of your team dynamic and find team synergy. By performing these exercises in any team you join or lead, you will directly empower members with agency for independent thinking and improve their abilities to work collaboratively. These exercises create the conditions for group flow by building trust and creating the psychological safety necessary for each member to fully turn up and lean in.

Finding team synergy feels a bit like playing the children's game 'Murder in the Dark'. Murder in the Dark is basically 'hide and seek' but *so* much more exciting because it's played at night. Hiders hide in the dark, and the seeker seeks with a torch. For older children, this game evokes that delicious combination of glee and fear – terror at being alone in the dark, anticipation of being found, and excitement at being discovered.

Shining the torch on the dynamic of a team can be a similar experience. It necessitates that all members are willing to lean into discomfort, be vulnerable and share the responsibility for how the group interacts. The payoff is a team where each individual feels seen, heard, understood, and empowered to contribute in ways that elevate both their own contributions and each other's.

As a part-time student completing a Masters of Organisation Dynamics, I participated in many activities designed to observe the dynamic of groups and hone my skills for tuning into team dynamics. One such experience was a Group Relations Conference (GRC), designed in the Tavistock Tradition.[1] A GRC is a five-day immersive learning experience, or a 'temporary learning organisation' in which delegates form and reform into groups of different size and composition over the five days. The sole purpose of the conference is to 'study the group dynamics as they occur', observing group life while also participating in it.

A bit like circular breathing is required to play the digeridoo, exploring group dynamics requires that participants master the art of simultaneous self-observation and participation. There is no other task, other than paying attention to how group members are interacting, as they are interacting. As you can imagine, GRCs are characterised by many, many long uncomfortable silences as anyone who says anything will be the focus for discussion and hypothesising for an entire session!

As uncomfortable as live group relations studies can be, they helped me understand that each group has its own dynamic that forms as a combination of the unique personalities, motivations and intentions of the individuals in the group. It forms as a projection of each

---

1 GRCs are usually open to the public and are held by different organisations around the world. They originate from the Tavistock Institute of Human Relations, based in London UK. If you are based in Australia and interested in discovering more, visit Group Relations Australia or the National Institute of Organisation Dynamics (NIODA).

individual's impression on the other – all of which happens silently and mostly subconsciously. If we can tap into and reveal some of those impressions, assumptions and individual motivations, actively listen, and find points of agreement, then we can create the psychological safety required for trust and respect to develop.

For most leaders and leadership teams, a five-day immersive GRC is impractical. Instead, the exercises described in this section can be performed in just a few hours each. They can be done in combination over a single team building day or separately over several days. These exercises invite teams to lean into conversations that invite curiosity, strengthen connection, and invoke calm. They create the conditions for flow so that teams can realise synergies and achieve peak performance. And anytime you feel your team start slipping back into dysfunction junction, they can be readministered to restore trust and rebuild respect.

GET REAL, GET CLOSE, GET BETTER

To find team synergy and create the conditions for group flow, teams need to:

- **Get Real** – diagnose team performance, discuss team dynamics, and decide on the preferred paradigm moving forward.

- **Get Close** – go deeper. Reveal unique capabilities and perspectives, appreciate how individuals value and create clarity on who owns what.

- **Get Better** – agree on purpose, align on principles, and resolve issues and conflicts as they occur.

All up, there are nine clusters of activities that teams can perform to positively shift the way they collaborate to innovate.

	DIAGNOSE Measure the dynamic	DISCUSS Identify strengths and opportunities	DECIDE Agree what needs to change
GET REAL	DIAGNOSE Measure the dynamic	DISCUSS Identify strengths and opportunities	DECIDE Agree what needs to change
GET CLOSE	SHARE Find what's unique	SEEK Elicit feedback	SOLVE Define who owns what
GET BETTER	PURPOSE Find your why	PRINCIPLES Align on how	PREVENTION Clear issues

The following chapters provide practical steps and how-to guides for leaders who want to do the work on their team dynamic and find team synergy. These exercises are empirically based and practically tested. They are simple to execute and deliver maximum impact.

But there is a catch. They require vulnerability and courage. These are trust- and respect-building exercises, and as we learned from Part III, there can be no trust without vulnerability. For these reasons, if you are going to lead your team through these exercises, your primary role is to create psychological safety.

Chapters 17, 18 and 19 outline the exercises to lead teams to synergy, while Chapter 20 describes how to facilitate these exercises in ways that create psychological safety required for vulnerability.

17

Get Real

Doctors can't solve health problems unless they diagnose the cause. Similarly, we can't work on the dynamic of the team unless we know what we're dealing with. To **Get Real**, we need to shine the torch into all the dark corners and reveal all the hiding spaces that are causing dysfunctional dynamics. We need to collectively discuss and diagnose the behaviours that are both helping and hindering team performance.

To get real requires honesty and courage. Honesty to share the truth, and courage to allow yourself to be vulnerable. If there are team dynamics holding us back in dysfunction junction, this is the time to bring it to light.

Getting Real involves three conversations – **Diagnose**, **Discuss** and **Decide**.

DIAGNOSE – MEASURE THE GROUP DYNAMIC

Peter Drucker is famous for saying 'what gets measured, gets managed'. The way people interact has been accused of being the 'fluffy stuff'. But using a diagnostic to measure behaviour turns the intangible into tangible and gives us a language and protocol for managing behaviour.

There are different diagnostic tools available for measuring group dynamics. YPO Forums (mentioned back in Chapter 14) have what's called a 'Forum Health Survey' which measures the degree to which Forum members are adhering to the success principles that support healthy Forum functioning.

In Chapter 2 we also heard about the Human Synergistics survival simulation that gives teams a way of measuring group behaviour and whether they've been able to achieve team synergy. While I am a big supporter of this measurement tool, you need to engage an accredited practitioner to use it. Not every team has the budget for this investment.

To address this challenge, I've developed the Team Synergy diagnostic (opposite) – a basic tool that anyone can download from my website and use. This diagnostic is based on The Five Interactions of a Team table, first outlined in Chapter 15.

You can download this diagnostic free from my website: www. stephaniebown.com/insights.

Make a copy for each team member and ask them to first individually fill it out before going into the discussion piece, outlined in the next section.

Team Synergy diagnostic

	Contribution	Voice	Listening	Questioning	Decision-making
	The proportion of individual contribution to the group	**The honesty and diversity of views shared**	**The degree to which ideas are understood and incorporated**	**The degree of curiosity, inquiry, and testing of ideas**	**The process for how decisions are ultimately made**
Team in Synergy **Overall Av. 2–3**	**Proportionate** Contribution is weighted to those with the most knowledge or experience based on the problem at hand Score: 3	**Diverse** A wide breadth and depth of ideas are actively sought and considered Score: 3	**Active** Members seek to both listen and confirm their understanding by paraphrasing and checking in Score: 3	**Exploratory** Questions expand on ideas and open further possibilities for new and different pathways Score: 3	**Consensus** Characterised by collective agreement on what will yield the best result for the business Score: 3
Functional Team **Overall Av. 1–2**	**Equal** There is conscious effort to share space equally and hear all voices Score: 2	**Honest** When shared, voice is honest, real and unbiased Score: 2	**Hearing** Listening is about hearing one another's views and allowing one's view to be influenced by others Score: 2	**Open** Questions invite discussion and debate to tease out variables on existing ideas Score: 2	**Compromise** Characterised by majority-rule, based on effective debate Score: 2
Dysfunctional Team **Overall Av. 0–1**	**Unbalanced** Dominant voices tend to fill the space Score: 1	**Masked** True opinions are hidden to fit in or avoid confrontation Score: 1	**Turn-taking** There is no listening, only waiting for one's turn to speak Score: 1	**Leading** Questions lead to foregone conclusions Score: 1	**Conformity** Characterised by conformity to hierarchy, rules and procedures Score: 1
Team Average					

DISCUSS – IDENTIFY STRENGTHS AND OPPORTUNITIES

Every team has things they do well and opportunities for improvement. This activity follows on from the **Diagnose** stage to make meaning and sense of how individuals experience the group.

When discussing team dynamics, it's important to set the scene by creating psychological safety. See Chapter 20 for more on this but here are some basic pointers.

FACILITATE A TEAM SYNERGY DIAGNOSTIC DEBRIEF

- Start the conversation by sharing your intent – that you are keen to help the team become a more healthy, high-functioning team.

- Make it safe by inviting honest viewpoints, recognising that everyone's experience of the group will be unique to them. Do not be surprised if there are vastly different experiences within the same team. This is an exercise in being vulnerable, which is a necessary part of building trust.

- Facilitate the conversation by surfacing everyone's scores. Start with the first dimension – i.e., 'contribution'. Ask everyone to share their score and write each score on a flipchart.

- For each interaction in the diagnostic (contribution, voice, listening, questioning, and decision-making), lead a discussion by asking:

  - What are the examples you're thinking about that led to these scores?

  - How did that example make you feel in the moment? How does it make you feel about the way we work together now?

  - What could we have done differently or better in those moments? What are some suggestions you have for improving the way we work moving forward?

- The more vulnerable individuals are willing to be, the more valuable the insights and learnings. A useful tool to bring into this conversation is the table on page 86 of this book. Who typically show up as sheep, lions, turtles or camels? This is a fun and safe way of owning the way individuals contribute to the dynamic.

- Summarise the conversation by drawing up on a flipchart two columns with the headings: *strengths* and *opportunities*. Ask the group to share what they perceive as the strengths of the team dynamic (how we help each other achieve high performance) and the opportunities for improvement (how we hinder performance).

- A great way to do this is to use the *Think, Pair, Share*[1] technique.

  - **Think** first – individuals note down what they heard were the team's strengths and opportunities for improvement.

  - **Pair** up – work with one other to collate your answers and come back to the group with their top two for each column.

  - **Share** – the answers from the pair with the broader group. Collate and summarise the list into three to five strengths, and three to five opportunities.

- Thank everyone for their contributions and honesty. Move onto the Decide conversation.

DECIDE - AGREE WHAT NEEDS TO CHANGE

When we **Decide**, we agree as a group what needs to change to improve the team dynamic.

The temptation at this stage is to create a laundry list of actions aimed at leveraging the strengths and realising the opportunities identified from the **Discuss** conversation. Resist this temptation! Choose just one thing.

In his 2014 book *The One Thing*, real estate entrepreneur Gary Keller argues that the key to success is to focus daily on the one thing that's most important for achieving your goal, rather than scattering yourself in several directions.

We can easily commit one thing to memory, and this increases the chances of making change. It's a positive cycle. Making a change as a result of a shared commitment leads to better performance, which

---

1 Think, Pair, Share ensures that everyone's voice is heard and considered. Individuals who are more introverted or quieter are forced to share, individuals who dominate are forced to listen. It is an efficient way to ask the group to do the work of drawing meaning from the discussion and boiling it down into a manageable number of areas to work on.

builds more trust and respect, which leads to stronger commitment and so on. The inverse is also true. Making a commitment and not doing it damages trust and respect, leading to worse performance.

> **Making a change as a result of a shared commitment leads to better performance, which builds more trust and respect, which leads to stronger commitment.**

The team interaction diagnostic (which you can download from my website) includes a space for you to pick one focus area, and to list the team habit you will commit to doing.

OUR FOCUS AREA FOR IMPROVEMENT AS A TEAM (PICK ONE):

Contribution	Voice	Listening	Questioning	Decision-making
The proportion of individual contribution to the group	The honesty and diversity of views shared	The degree to which ideas are understood and incorporated	The degree of curiosity, inquiry, and testing of ideas	The process for how decisions are ultimately made

List this new habit and make a commitment to practicing it. Make sure you list a habit as an observable behaviour – something you can actually see others do or say – and not something vague and general. Check out the examples below (pick one):

- Example *contribution* habit: 'On shared topics, all voices are heard by each sharing our opinion using "yes and", or "yes but".'

- Example *voice* habit: 'We take a moment to reflect on and write our own views down before sharing with the broader group.'

- Example *listening* habit: 'Demonstrate understanding by paraphrasing and checking in, before we share another view.'

- Example *questioning* habit: 'We ask "what else" at least three times when problem-solving.'

- Example *decision-making* habit: 'We first agree on the problem to be solved before we start working on the solution.'

This is by no means an exhaustive list of potential new habits to address each interaction dynamic. Each team will bring their own flavour and language to the task.

Once you've committed to the one thing, remember to bring that new habit into every single interaction with members of that team for at least the next 30 days. As the leader of the process, you need to lead the way on this. Do whatever it takes for you to remind yourself! Make it the first point on every agenda. Make it your screen saver. Post it on the meeting room wall. Set a calendar reminder. It generally takes 30 days of considered practice to adopt a new habit. Once you've done that, redo the exercise. Find another habit to focus on. Rinse and repeat!

The leadership team of a Denmark-based pharmaceutical company that I worked with recognised that their main challenge was Voice – withholding individual views when it was unpopular or could generate disagreement. They admitted that they were guilty of *passive disagreement*. They were agreeing with each other in meetings, only to disagree outside the meeting, or having the 'meeting after the meeting'. They decided to switch to *active disagreement*, to share disagreements openly in meetings, and to commit to one course of action regardless of their initial stance.

To address this, they drew on inspiration from Amazon founder Jeff Bezos, who famously created the 'disagree and commit' philosophy. According to Bezos, most decisions are reversible, two-way doors. Those types of decisions can use a lightweight process to save on time. 'Disagree and commit' invites teams to have open disagreements, discuss options, commit based on the best guess, and test and learn – all without fear of failure or blame. Not everyone needs to agree, but once all available options are weighted, they need to commit and execute.

'Disagree and commit' became the new mantra of my Denmark-based leadership team. There were bolstered by their success at adopting a new habit, so they agreed to try a 'new habit of the month' to stack up their commitments to living the company values. In this way they helped themselves and each other be role models for the values, which had an enormously positive impact on company culture.

18

Get Close

To **Get Close** we must go deeper. This means sharing more of ourselves, getting to know one another so that we can appreciate the full range of capabilities and perspectives we have available in the team.

Learning more about each other builds *familiarity*, one of Keith Sawyer's (2007) 10 conditions for group flow. 'By studying many different work teams, psychologists have found that familiarity increases productivity and decision-making effectiveness.' (p. 40).

It also supports the *blending of egos*, another condition for group flow. By learning more about each other, members may start to anticipate each other's responses, actively seek input where individual strengths and talents are required, and move together in ways that align or complement ways of working.

To **Get Close**, teams must **Share**, **Seek** and **Solve**.

SHARE – FIND WHAT'S UNIQUE

Familiarity can be fast-tracked by learning more about what makes each member of the group tick. There are literally hundreds of ways teams can learn more about each other – from going on team building adventure camps to simply sharing their resumes. The three suggested here are ways I've successfully helped groups connect on a deeper level that cost little in terms of time and budget yet created maximum impact.

Values

Our values are instilled in us from birth, inherited from our caregivers by observing their actions and words. In this way, values are transmitted through generations as part of our cultural programming. They colour our perception of the world, giving us the measuring stick for what we deem to be positive, negative, ethical, immoral, enjoyable or distasteful.

By learning about the values of our colleagues, we can understand what is truly important to them, what drives them, why they fight for some things and let other things slide. Values are very personal, so require vulnerability to share, which builds trust and fosters greater empathy.

> **By learning about the values of our colleagues, we can understand what is truly important to them, what drives them, why they fight for some things and let other things slide.**

One group of executives I worked with ran this exercise and learned that one of their members lived in a slum in India until the age of 12. He then won a scholarship to a prestigious school, founded his own business, and moved his entire family to Australia. This team had worked together for several years and never knew his incredible story. It explained his enthusiasm for equal opportunity, for investment in education for employees, and his overwhelming generosity – characteristics that at times had seemed frivolous during lean moments at the company. He gained their respect and it became a more inclusive team from that moment on.

FACILITATE A VALUES DISCOVERY SESSION

To lead a team through a values discovery session, get your team together and ask them to follow these steps. You can use the Values Activity provided as an addendum to Part IV:

- Think about when you've been at your happiest and most fulfilled – a 'peak' experience in your life. What values were being felt and expressed at that time?

- Use the Values Activity (addendum) or simply ask them to list as many values that come to mind. Examples are – adventure, courage, curiosity, creativity, family, fitness, gratitude, honesty, leadership, quality, punctuality, structure, trust, respect, empathy.

- Ask each individual to boil the list down to their Top 5. List these in priority order, with #1 being the most important.

- Define each value – give it a name and write one sentence about what your chosen value means to you. Different words mean different things to people so it's important to define what your value means to you.

- Write each value on a separate Post-it note.

- Share these one by one with the team – posting all the values on a flipchart. As you share each value, share a story about where this value came from in your life or why it's particularly important to you.

- Once everyone has shared, identify where the group has similar values. Discuss how these might be showing up now in the way this group works together. This is a great moment to highlight where the overlaps are between the group's shared values and the company values. Quite often there is significant overlap, particularly if the organisation is focussed on people and culture.

- Identify where individuals are unique in their chosen values. Discuss how their uniqueness adds richness and complexity to the way this group interacts.

- Thank everyone for their contributions and honesty.

Strengths

Strengths are people's natural talents, finely honed over years of practice. The strengths-based proposition, developed by Gallup, is that high performance and personal excellence can only be achieved by maximising strengths and utilising them as much as possible, never solely by fixing weaknesses (Rath, 2007). Gallup research comprehensively demonstrates that employees who know and use their strengths at work are more engaged, productive and effective than those who don't.

Gallup has surveyed more than 10 million people worldwide. Their research shows that people who have the opportunity to focus on their strengths are six times more likely to be engaged in their job, and three times more likely to report excellent quality of life in general.[1]

Sharing strengths within teams achieves multiple advantages:

- It's energising to learn about and talk about one's own strengths.

- It gives the team an opportunity to share responsibilities based on strengths.

- It directs the energy for learning and development in the areas of strengths.

- It helps teams understand how they have complementary strengths and can support each other in the achievement of shared goals.

The best way to adopt a strengths-based language and mindset is to use a diagnostic to measure individual strengths and share these with each other. The Gallup organisation offers the CliftonStrengths Assessment – which anyone can order and purchase online for a reasonable fee. Alternatively, the Values in Action or VIA Character Strengths survey is a free online survey that is scientifically validated, developed by The Positive Psychology Center at the University of Pennsylvania. By completing this survey, you contribute data to the database that adds to the validity and reliability of the survey.

---

1   https://www.gallup.com/cliftonstrengths/en/253790/science-of-cliftonstrengths.aspx

FACILITATE A STRENGTHS DISCOVERY SESSION

Before the session, invite everyone to complete a strengths-based diagnostic assessment and bring their results to the session.

- Mention that the goal of the session is to recognise and appreciate what makes us good at what we do, and to discover how we can leverage complementary strengths.

- One by one, ask everyone to share their top five strengths *and* one way they are using each strength in their role right now.

- Similar to the values activity, highlight where there are shared strengths, and where there are unique strengths, appreciating the value that diversity brings.

- An adjunct activity could be to ask each individual to meet one-on-one (speed-dating style) in five-minute rounds. In each round, they each provide one suggestion to the other for how they can leverage a strength in a new way in service to the team.

- At the end of every round, come back together as a group and ask each individual to reveal one suggestion they will put into action in service of the team's goals.

Personality

A popular activity for teams to get to know each other better is to use a personality profiling tool like DiSC or Myers-Briggs Type Indicator (MBTI) to reveal the personality characteristics of individuals. These tools are popular for good reason – they help us appreciate and value differences in personality. Personality, like strengths, is inherited and shaped through formative experiences. We cannot change our personality but we can adapt how we express our personality at work and in life.

Learning about the personalities of colleagues will help you understand their preferences for ways of working. An important personality dimension to teamwork and collaboration is one's preference towards introversion or extroversion. Typically, dominant members are extroverts, while silent members are introverts but of course there are exceptions to this rule. This highlights the importance of allowing contribution and voice regardless of preferences.

When team members have vastly different personality profiles they will typically find it harder to get along. Conversely, same types find it easier to get along. But if we only recruit for same, we land in group-think. Having vastly different types of thinkers in a single team is a huge advantage when it comes to fostering creativity and innovation.

The only challenge with these types of activities is that personality is relatively fixed, and labelling someone as a particular personality type can pigeonhole them in ways that don't capture the richness of their uniqueness. I am a supporter of personality profile tools (I am accredited in MBTI myself) but I recognise that they have also been done to death and have limitations in their impact on improving performance.

SEEK – ELICIT FEEDBACK

It's one thing to share more about ourselves and another thing entirely to understand how we are perceived by others. Eliciting feedback to close the gap between our intentions and others' perceptions is a criti-cal step in building team synergy.

Normalising a feedback culture within teams is a proven method-ology for improving team performance. For this reason, learning how to give and receive feedback is a core component of any leadership program that I deliver to my clients and a topic with its own chapter in my first book, *Purpose, Passion and Performance*.

When colleagues give each other behaviour-based feedback which highlights the positives and appreciates strengths, they instantly improve relationships, build trust, and create psychological safety.

> **When colleagues give each other behaviour-based feedback which highlights the positives and appreciates strengths, they instantly improve relationships, build trust, and create psychological safety.**

Equally important is receiving feedback – asking for feedback and responding positively to it – regardless of the content of the message. Feedback is a gift. When someone you respect takes the time and effort to be honest and share their perception of how you can show up better at work, they are taking an interpersonal risk to help you. By thanking them for their gift, you make it safe. You create calm by sending signals that people in your team are respected and that their voice matters.

FACILITATE THE FEEDBACK ROUNDING EXERCISE

To normalise a culture of feedback get your team together for regular (ideally quarterly) feedback rounding exercises. Here's how it's done:

- Working in pairs, each team member will have a 10-minute 'round' – speed-dating style – with every other team member in which they will each share at least three observed strengths (things I see you do well) to one piece of constructive feedback (an opportunity I see for you is...).

- In each 10-minute round, each team member has five minutes each. All participants take notes on the feedback given to them.

- Run a series of 10-minute rounds – up to 90 minutes (everyone tires a little at this point). If your team is large and you need more rounds, have a break and start again. Ensure everyone thanks their partner at the end of each round.

- Keep the energy light. Play music, use a bell or sound to signal when rounds are finished.

- Conduct a debrief with the whole group asking how it felt to receive positive and constructive feedback.

- Ask each person to share with the whole group – what themes they picked up, what others see as their top three strengths, and what others see as their greatest opportunity for improvement.

- Capture each person's key recognised strength and key opportunity on a flipchart and put it in a shared workspace (in the office or online) so that everyone can continue to appreciate strengths and support each other's development.

The feedback rounding exercise is a team hygiene exercise. The two-way nature of the interaction puts everyone on a level playing field regardless of positional authority and helps to build a stronger sense of appreciation for the value that everyone brings. It's also an opportunity to clear any tensions that may be building.

This exercise works well on its own, but it can be significantly elevated when accompanied by a behavioural diagnostic – which adds quantitative 'hard' data to the qualitative 'soft' data shared by colleagues. For my executive clients, I use the Human Synergistics 360-degree feedback version of the Life-Styles Inventory (LSI), which provides a visual representation of the degree to which leaders are demonstrating both constructive and defensive behaviours – as perceived by the self and others. If I use this diagnostic, individuals receive their reported feedback in a one-on-one debrief before coming together to share their results as a group. Having the diagnostic data allows us to measure and track changes that leaders make over time, which creates far more accountability for behavioural change.

Feedback – whether qualitative or quantitative – facilitates *open communication* – one of the 10 key conditions for group flow. Keith Sawyer cites the work of Stefan Falk, the Vice President of Strategic Business Innovation at Ericsson, who read *Flow* and redesigned the company to make flow the core of its philosophy.

> *Every manager was required to meet with each employee six times a year in elaborate feedback sessions lasting over an hour. When Falk moved to Green Cargo, a large Scandinavian transport company, he went even further – requiring monthly meetings between managers and employees, intensive sessions that are something like executive coaching. In 2004, Green Cargo turned a profit for the first time in its 120-year government-owned history, and the CEO gives much of the credit to Falk's flow strategies. (Sawyer, 2022, p. 42)*

SOLVE – DEFINE WHO OWNS WHAT

To be enabled to perform, all humans need two basic things: role clarity and goal clarity. Having role clarity and goal clarity creates the conditions for *being in control*, a key factor that enables group flow.

Role clarity is about knowing what's expected of me and how I fit in. **Goal clarity** is about understanding the level of performance expected of me.

Typically, job descriptions provide role clarity, while annual goals and key performance indicators (KPIs) provide goal clarity. These two assets work together to provide individuals with clarity on what's expected of them.

In teams, it's not enough to understand what individuals are responsible for. Teams are different from groups in that they have shared goals. Being *better together* emerges when there is shared understanding of what the team's collective goals are, as well as clear accountability for who does what.

USE RACI TO CREATE GOAL AND ROLE CLARITY

One effective method for this is to use the RACI methodology.

RACI is an acronym for:

R – Responsible – who needs to contribute to doing the work?

A – Accountable – who is ultimately accountable for the work?

C – Consult – who has expertise that can help?

I – Inform – who is impacted and needs to be kept informed?

To use RACI – you need to start with the shared team goals.

A company strategy or 'one-page plan' (if you have one)[1] sets out the goals for an executive team. This needs to be replicated for every team in an organisation – helping teams at every level develop a collective understanding of shared accountabilities.

---

1 For more on building a clear and actionable one-page-plan, see Part IV of my first book, *Purpose, Passion and Performance.*

For each goal, one person must be assigned *Accountability*. This should ideally be just one person – so that there is no confusion about who is driving the activity.

But that person does not work alone – they need to work with those *Responsible* – individuals who must collaborate with the one *Accountable* to deliver the result.

To *Consult* is to provide input because you have capability that can help.

To *Inform* is to be kept in the loop because the actions from that activity will have an impact on your activities.

A CAVEAT ON GETTING CLOSE – HOW CLOSE IS TOO CLOSE?

There is a caveat to getting close. When groups become too familiar, it reduces the opportunity for flow by minimising novelty and unpredictability. The team maxes out on innovation potential because they know too much about each other and think too similarly.

Executive teams which remain the same for many years running may become stale and insular in their thinking, negatively impacting their organisation's performance. This dynamic can be changed by changing up the environment and having new experiences (such as going on a retreat), bringing in new team members, or changing up the roles they play. To remain adaptive in changing market conditions, sometimes this necessitates a change in team membership.

Some examples are:

- The CEO of Swisse Wellness, Radek Sali (while they were still privately owned), transitioned the serving CFO to the COO role when he recognised that the company needed a seasoned decision-maker to improve the supply chain. Simultaneously he recruited a new CFO who had the experience necessary to prepare the business for sale.[1]

---

1 You can learn more about Radek's incredible story in his book *How to Build a Billion-Dollar Business*.

- The CEO of an executive leadership team who had the same 10 members for five consecutive years created a new option for executives who were ready to step out of executive responsibilities, but not ready to retire. He graduated them to strategic specialists, leading special strategic projects such as mergers or new product categories. Simultaneously, he promoted four members from the second-tier leadership level to executive membership. This happened in a year in which a new company vision was being developed, so that the new members could bring fresh thinking to the table.

- The board of a tech company has a compulsory three-year tenure for the Chair with no option to renew. The Chair may step into a non-executive director role or opt out of the board once the term is up. This ensures fresh thinking is installed at the highest level on a semi-regular basis.

- YPO groups have an age-out criteria – once Forum members reach a certain age, they graduate to the next level called YPO Gold and join a new Forum. This process makes space for new members to join existing Forums and ensures that Forums are composed of members who are all at a similar age and stage.

19

Get Better

To **Get Better** is to create a platform for growth. To continuously improve, we need to set clear benchmarks for performance, and we need to help each other be accountable to those standards.

To *get better*, teams can fast-track their route to high performance. This means speeding up their stages of group development.

Psychologist Bruce Tuckman first introduced the stages of group development in the 1960s. These were:

- **Forming:** The group comes together to understand their purpose, mission, roles and goals. There is an instant dynamic that evolves from first impressions. This is an exciting time as we discover similarities between us.

- **Storming:** We start to discover the differences and points where we don't agree. Power struggles and conflict can occur as we try to align on who does what and when.

- **Norming:** We find points of alignment. Agree on shared purpose, goals, principles and values. We gain confidence that we can achieve the mission.

- **Performing:** We are actively achieving our goals, building confidence and trust in the group with each encounter.

- **Adjourning:** The phase of work is over or there is turnover of team members in the group. The cycle starts again.

If we recognise that these are natural, normal stages of development, we can adopt strategies to actively fast-track the whole cycle. The aim is to reach the performing stage as quickly as possible.

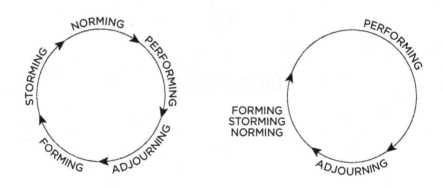

To get better and fast-track the norming stage involves three conversations – Purpose, Principles and Prevention.

Anytime there is a change to a team, these team activities should be re-done. A new member means this is an entirely new group. Instead of expecting the new team member to just 'fit in' with what is already in place, a better way is to re-set the purpose and principles, and to relearn how to prevent conflict. Doing this gives the new member of the group an opportunity to belong, instead of just 'fitting in' to the group status quo.

PURPOSE – FIND YOUR WHY

Purpose is a powerful tool for leaders. When harnessed at the organisational, team and individual level, it has the power to connect whole organisations, align teams and inspire people.

Your purpose defines your why – how you add value. It creates meaning and significance to the work people in your team come together to do every day. It answers key questions like how are we helping? What difference are we making? Why should anyone care?

| Your purpose defines your why – how you add value.

It is common practice these days for organisational purpose to be defined and stated on its website and communications assets. It is less common for *teams* to know *their* why, and how they support the mission of the organisation. For a team to function, they must know their purpose. This is as true for leadership teams (boards, executive teams, senior leadership teams) as it is for functional teams (sales, operations, finance, etc.), and for special project teams or committees.

A galvanising purpose is one that meets three criteria. They need to be:

- **Aspirational and enduring** – it is our North Star, we are always reaching but never quite get there.

- **Short and sharp** – no more than seven words (plus or minus two), so that we can hold them in our memory.

- **Specific and clear** – it speaks directly to what we do. They are not vague and general like, 'Making the world a better place'.

(For more detail on creating your organisational purpose, refer to Chapter IV of my first book, *Purpose, Passion and Performance*).

DEFINE YOUR TEAM PURPOSE

- Start by explaining that being clear on our why and defining our purpose gives us clarity on how our work is meaningful and adds value to the organisation.

- Revisit the organisation purpose statement (if you have one). Point out that we will be working on our team why – how our team serves this purpose.

- Mention that our purpose statement must meet these criteria:
  - aspirational and enduring
  - short and sharp (7 +/- 2 words)
  - specific and clear.

- Give everyone five minutes to first individually write down why this team exists in no more than nine words.

- Ask each individual to share and capture each statement visually (up on a flipchart, or online format).

- Underline the key words and statements that everyone agrees are important.
- Facilitate a conversation about how we consolidate this to a single sentence.
- Thank the group for their input, and encourage everyone to come back to this purpose anytime they need to make key decisions.

This process may take a little time and require several iterations. Stick with it. Leaning into the discomfort of not having an immediate or obvious solution allows the team to work the problem and innovate.

NB: You can use an AI tool like ChatGPT to do the heavy lifting, but make sure you apply your own language filters and add your own creative twist.

PRINCIPLES – ALIGN ON HOW

Every group has its norms – implicit expectations for working together. The work of creating great cultures is about making the implicit, explicit. It's the work of setting norms and expectations for behaviours that align with the team or organisation's values and to which everyone both agrees with and holds each other accountable.

Culture is the outcome of values in action. When our behaviours match our values, we build trust and respect.

> **Culture is the outcome of values in action. When our behaviours match our values, we build trust and respect.**

For teams to have a chance of living up to each other's expectations regarding behaviour, they need to make these expectations explicit. Setting principles enables us to avoid the BANS (referred to in Chapter 8) – biases, assumptions, norms and self-limiting beliefs – while also creating a solid foundation for teamwork.

YPO Forum groups have a specific set of norms that they set clear expectations against and renew every year. Each Forum creates a Forum Norms document – an explicit agreement that everyone must sign. This document outlines expectations against the Forum success principles of confidentiality, commitment, meeting structure, communication protocol, leadership, membership, renewal and shared mission.

Boards set codes of conduct and terms of reference that provide clear boundaries for behaviour and input required by directors.

Similarly, leadership teams should set their expectations for each other in explicit terms. A great way of approaching this is using the organisation's values as a starting point for the conversation. How they behave should be in alignment with the values that direct and guide all behaviour in the workplace.

SET CLEAR PRINCIPLES FOR WORKING TOGETHER

Start with the organisation's values and ask each individual to write down what 'living the values' as a leader and member of this team looks like, in practical terms.

Write each value at the top of a flipchart and ask everyone to share their points. Avoid repetition by adding only new points each time they are shared, under the relevant headings.

Underline what are the most important behaviours – try to boil these down to a manageable set of seven to nine specific expectations that guide behaviour.

If you use an AI tool like ChatGPT then be sure to apply your own language filters and creative flair to the final set of statements.

Ask everyone in the group if they all agree to these expectations. Give permission to everyone in the group to hold each other accountable, anytime they are not demonstrated or adhered to.

Call out examples of individuals who've demonstrated a value in action at the start or end of every team interaction. Positive feedback – noticing when people do the right thing and acknowledging it – is THE greatest behavioural change lever a leader can pull.

Positive feedback is far more motivating than negative feedback – calling out when people don't follow the protocols or when they make mistakes. While negative feedback is a necessary evil (we can't let the standards drop), we gain far greater performance outcomes when we weight feedback on the positive. A good ratio to aim for is 4:1 – four positive call-outs to each negative call-out.

PREVENTION – CLEAR ISSUES

Conflict happens. There will be points of disagreement, frustrations, words spoken that are perceived as insulting, biased or incompetent. There are typically two categories of conflict – **relationship conflict** or **task conflict**. Every relationship in work and life experiences conflict at some point. Task conflict can happen when there are misunderstandings about who does what, when strategies are not working, when projects are not progressing, or when we are failing to achieve expected results. The issue is not whether conflict happens, but how team members resolve it.

Relationships can grow from conflict – it doesn't have to be a negative thing. In fact, overcoming conflict deepens and strengthens relationships. Anyone who has sustained a happy marriage for many years can attest to this!

> **Relationships can grow from conflict – it doesn't have to be a negative thing.**

What most teams lack however is a process for resolving issues and conflict. Instead of addressing the issue directly, many avoid confrontation for fear of damaging their relationship. When there is not enough psychological safety in the group, the interpersonal risk is too high. In these circumstances, individuals take a passive or indirect approach, discussing it with anyone *except* the person it is about. This in fact is more damaging than addressing the issue directly.

Committing to an **Issues Clear** process is a great way to give teams confidence that they can handle any conflict that will inevitably spring up along the way. Practicing first on minor issues is a great way to systematically build psychological safety and relationship resilience. Making this a regular step in team meetings is also a healthy way of resolving issues rather than letting them stack up and fester. Don't wait for the annual engagement survey to find out that your team is disengaged – surface any issues as part of your regular meeting habits.

The *Issues Clear* process outlined below is an effective resolution strategy that ensures involved parties feel heard and understood, and that we move quickly from a problem mindset to a solution mindset.

Issues Clear process

Issue and impact (person A)	What I heard (person B)	Issues list (use together)
• The issue or challenge I wish to raise is ... (the facts) • The impact this had (on me/on others/ on the business) • What I think we need a resolution on is ...	• I heard you say your issue or challenge is ... • The impact was ... • Have I heard you correctly?	• What we agree needs to be solved
←——————————→ **Swap roles and repeat as necessary**		**Then move to GROW to problem solve**

FACILITATE AN ISSUES CLEAR

- Start by sharing the Issues Clear process pictured above. Explain the process, that each individual (Person A) who has an issue will be asked to share it specifically using the steps outlined.

- The person or people to whom the issue is directed (Person B) will also be asked to respond using the very specific steps outlined.

- Explain that it is important we hear and understand each other's perspectives – which is why we will follow the process precisely.

- If there are multiple issues to raise, we will repeat the process until they are all shared and heard. Only after Person B has responded to Person A, will we swap roles (if necessary) and allow the process to repeat.

- As we agree on what needs to be solved, each time we will add that to an **Issues List**. Write these down on a flipchart as the conversation progresses.
- Sometimes, just being heard and acknowledged is enough to resolve the issues. If it is resolved, we will not add it to the Issues List. If the issue is on the list, and needs to be worked through, move to GROW (see below) to problem-solve.
- Address each issue, one by one.
- Depending on the depth and complexity of the problems to be solved, this may necessitate a separate conversation. If that is the case, ensure you schedule the time and place for GROW conversations before you finish the session.

HOW DO WE GROW?

GROW is a coaching methodology introduced by Sir John Whitmore in his book *Coaching for Performance* in 1992. It has since been adopted as a foundational method as part of the *Australian Institute for Executive Coaching* program. It is a versatile method that can be applied across multiple contexts, such as customer service, team planning or in problem-solving.

GROW is an acronym for four stages of a conversation:

G – Goal: What do you want to achieve?
R – Reality: What is the situation?
O – Options: What are your options?
W – Way Forward: What actions will you take?

As an issue resolution tool, this process quickly moves teams from focussing on the problem to focussing on the solution. It asks for input on the definition of the problem to be solved, and it also asks for input on options for resolution – seeking a range of options and activating creative thinking before zoning in on a specific way forward.

For more on GROW and how to use it, check out Chapter 9 of my book *Purpose, Passion and Performance*, or pick up a copy of *Coaching for Performance*.

20

Create safety - be a facilitator

There is one key factor that determines whether the team activities designed to enhance team dynamics (described in the previous three chapters) will be a success, and that is how well they are facilitated.

Facilitation is a mode of operating. It is distinct from other modes like managing, directing, speaking, coaching, training, mentoring or counselling. Each of these modes has their own distinct behavioural template. In facilitation mode, we do not deliver content, but instead frame conversations, draw the content from the group, and work with the group to consolidate inputs and agree on outputs.

When facilitating, we are creating the spaces for people to work through challenges and solve problems. Facilitators provide containment. They actively remain calm and composed, and are role models of vulnerability and keepers of the process. They set the tone for the conversations by themselves being an example of positive interactive dynamics – setting clear objectives, inviting input, demonstrating deep listening, asking questions and consolidating outputs.

> **When facilitating, we are creating the spaces for people to work through challenges and solve problems. Facilitators provide containment.**

It is an especially important mode when facilitating sessions on team synergy because the team themselves must work on how they are each contributing to their own dynamics. It must be safe to step up and own their part, question and challenge each other directly, and feel that they will not be making career-limiting moves by raising issues on ways of working that may be hindering team performance. These conversations are risky business for leaders, and therefore require sensitive management.

I first fell in love with the power of facilitation during my formative professional years as a management consultant at Nous Group. One of my projects was to support a team of facilitators delivering a pilot leadership program for a federal government agency. If successful, this pilot would be rolled out across hundreds of staff, so getting it right was paramount. The team included Lea Thorpe, Tim Pence, Kim Boekeman and Christine Wilson, who've all enjoyed long professional careers in the crafts of leading and facilitating since those days in the early 2000s.

While each facilitator had their own style, common between them was their mastery for rapidly creating the space for connection and deep conversation. It was astounding to notice how seasoned senior bureaucrats would lean in, listen, and deep-dive into conversations with peers on personal challenges, professional fears, painful regrets and hopes for change.

I was deeply impressed and quickly paid attention to the structures and strategies these masters of facilitation used to create safety, set the tone and contain the space. The sections following describe some of the most important techniques I've learned about facilitation from the best. When I don't follow these steps, I can tell. People aren't as vulnerable or engaged, and we don't find the depth of connection that breeds lasting trust. Use these techniques and you are guaranteed to strengthen the bonds of trust and respect to enable a more collaborative and inclusive team environment.

WORK THE PROCESS

For any workshop or meeting there are three key stages: pre-workshop, during and after. The processes outlined below contribute to creating a calm and safe in environment in which people willingly participate.

Pre-workshop

Walking into the room knowing what to expect is the first step towards creating calm.

Let people know in advance what's coming up by sharing a pre-session email.

This might include:

- the objectives of the session
- the attendee list (usually obvious by looking at the email list)
- pre-reading or preparation questions
- the agenda with basic timeframes for each session
- an invitation for questions or concerns to be raised directly with you.

While you are not expected to be an event or logistics manager, ensure you secure an appropriate space for your session that encourages open conversation and a more relaxed vibe. A fishbowl boardroom may not be the best place for an honest and vulnerable team discussion! In fact, any boardroom-style table, unless it's for a board meeting, can feel a bit stitched up. The best set-up is a circle of chairs with no table in the middle – group therapy style! Or at the very least, a room with lots of natural light. Ideally – for conversations that require space and time – move the team to a different location outside the office or usual meeting space. This often stimulates a different way of engaging from the outset.

During the workshop

Regardless of whether your session runs for a few hours or a full day, these are the keys to a successful session.

Set the scene: Start by welcoming the group, sharing the purpose and objectives of the session, and briefly running through the agenda. This gets everyone's heads in the game and is an important framing piece. Never assume people have read the agenda, done the pre-reading or even know why they are there!

Remove distractions: Ask if anyone is on call for anything urgent happening outside the room. If not, ask them to please turn off notifications, and close laptops (if they are not required for the session). This sends a signal that paying attention is a sign of respect and that unless there is a real reason, they need to contain unnecessary distractions.

My tip for this is to provide good-quality notebooks and pens in sessions and make a point that today will be about taking notes 'analogue' style. Any devices – phones, laptops – creates disconnection. The whole point of a workshop is to connect with the people in the room. Do not underestimate how quickly you can lose a whole group when just one person checks their phone or decides to respond to an email in the middle of a conversation! When phones are picked up, we are telling the people we are in front of that they are not the most important person to us in this moment.

Role model vulnerability: Set the tone for honesty and openness by sharing a story about why this conversation today matters. Make yourself as vulnerable as you can be – especially if you are the HiPPO in the room (Highest Paid Person in the Office). The key to being vulnerable is sharing the emotions you attach to your story. Sharing that you are feeling emotions like guilt, shame, fear, frustration or regret demonstrate that you are willing to be your 'true self' in this team. What you are doing is starting a cascade of openness, something Daniel Coyle refers to in his book *The Culture Code* as the 'vulnerability loop'.

The vulnerability loop works as follows:

- Person A shows their vulnerability.
- Person B recognises this, and shows their vulnerability.
- Now Person A recognises Person B responded in kind.
- Trust between Person A and B becomes stronger.

How vulnerable can you be? The basic test is how comfortable you are. To be vulnerable, you will need to lean into discomfort. Go to the place you feel uncomfortable yet maintain calm. This is where calm really comes into play. If you can be uncomfortable, yet contained and calm, you're being an adult! Congratulations!

> **To be vulnerable, you will need to lean into discomfort.**

After sharing your story, invite each participant to share what they'd like to get out of the session or why this session is important to them. List their ideas, concerns or contributions on a flipchart and mention that you will revisit this at the end of the session.

Each working session has four parts: As mentioned previously, facilitators do not deliver content, they draw it from the group. Lynne Cazaley is the author of *Leader as Facilitator* (2016) and uses a *Facilitator 4 Step* for meetings and conversations:

1. Facts and evidence – What do we know?
2. Discussion and opinion – What do we think?
3. Ideas and opportunity – What could we do?
4. Actions and commitment – What will we do?

The key with facilitation is that the content comes from the group, not from the facilitator. Facilitators frame the conversations, draw out the inputs, consolidate the thinking, and collaborate to agree on the outputs or 'next steps' for each conversation. This is a process of creating shared understanding and consensus on the best path forward so that there is ultimate buy-in.

Extra tips for building safety during these working sessions are:

- Capture inputs visually – on a flipchart or whiteboard (or relevant online version). This demonstrates that what people say is important and valuable.

- Manage the contribution in the room – subtly close down dominant voices and invite in silent ones. Ensure all voices are heard by asking something like 'thanks for your contribution.

That's one opinion – let's hear from others…' or 'That's useful, thanks. Who has a different opinion or idea?'

- Use questions to ask people to go deeper: 'Tell me more about that?', 'How did that make you feel?', 'Why was that important to you?'. Not everyone knows how to be vulnerable – your questions can help them get there.

- Manage the time. If a conversation will run overtime, check that others are OK with that. Demonstrate that you're actively managing time, not letting it run away from you.

- Use your own body language as a cue for listening. Sit on the chair and lean in when it's time to listen. Stand when it's time to capture outcomes. You set the tone with what you say and how you move every minute of the session.

Close with gratitude: Closing well is important. If we started the workshop with emotional connection and vulnerability, we need to close the boundary around that. Closing well involves asking each member of the group to share their answers to one or all of these questions:

- What they are thankful for?

- What did they learn from the discussion?

- What is their key takeaway/personal commitment from the conversation?

This is almost my favourite part of the workshop because people always surprise me. Briefly check back in on the objectives listed at the start of the day and whether we've achieved those. If not – make a point that you will park them for next time or follow up directly.

Post the workshop

The outputs from workshops are valuable. They are the thinking and agreements made between teams that can be incorporated in future work or revisited in future discussions.

If you've done a good enough job of writing notes on flipcharts and whiteboards, capture photos of these and distribute. Otherwise, take notes or delegate this task to someone in the group who has the time and capacity to do so.

Distribute the outputs (via photo or typed form) to the attendees, thanking them for their input and mentioning how you will use this data for future work or conversations.

WORK ON YOURSELF

Your mental and emotional state will set the tone for how people connect more than any process or technique, and more than the words you say. The reason people still crave in-person experiences is because there is so much communicated through body language and presence that cannot be transmitted online.

> **Your mental and emotional state will set the tone for how people connect more than any process or technique, and more than the words you say.**

When working on high-stakes or high-stress moments, whether it be facilitating or simply working in a team, how you show up will make a significant difference to the team's capacity to maintain calm, find synergy and perform to their best.

When I started pursuing more professional speaking as an adjunct to my practice, I decided to skill-up on the art and science of this mode, so I booked myself into Matt Church's *Speakership* program. There was one phrase that Matt repeated over and over throughout his three-day program that stuck with me. I draw on this often in moments where I need to find my own sense of calm:

'State matters more than script.'

While speaking is different to facilitating, they are very close cousins. I now repeat this mantra to myself whenever I am walking into a space where I feel the pressure to perform, or in high-stakes moments.

Stress is contagious, but so is calm. Actively finding flow is an act of containment. Containment of the self, containment of the space, containment of others.

On containment, containers and being contained

No...this is not about Tupperware. Or shipping. Or getting locked up.

It's about *psychological* containment, or the ability to hold and manage emotions, thoughts and experiences in a safe and constructive way.

Psychoanalyst Wilfred Bion originally coined the term *containment* to describe the capacity to internally manage troubling thoughts, feelings and behaviours.

It is a psychological process through which we create a sense of safety and stability within ourselves, allowing us to navigate challenges with more ease and empathy. Think of it as a container that holds emotions, preventing them from overwhelming us or spilling over into other areas of our lives.

Containment is what parents do when they hold their crying children. They literally hold their child and interpret their emotions for them – is it pain? Hunger? Sadness? Fear? What do you need? And then they fix it with a Band-Aid, a kiss, a talk or a tickle. Our mothers and fathers do this until such a time as we can hold our own emotions and sort ourselves out.

As adults, when we feel strong emotions, we need to put them somewhere. Learning self-containment means being able to hold your own emotions, yourself. Or finding a suitable container elsewhere to process them – a friend, a therapist, a trusted colleague.

To contain is to lead – yourself and others – so that we can work through the inevitable emotions that are conjured every time we work through what can seem like impossible goals in impossible times. Which, nowadays, is almost always.

'Be calm' hacks

How do you do this in the heat of the moment when the pressure is on? Over the years I've developed some 'deep calm' hacks – rapid on-the-spot techniques to maintain a steady state in times of anxiety when working in high-pressure moments – either in workshops, on a stage, or supporting teams through challenging conversations.

Consider these:

- **Breath:** In the moment, simply focus on how you're breathing. Take longer, slower, deeper breaths. Slightly constrict the back of your throat so you can hear the breath moving in and out. Feel how this changes your whole physiology.

- **Mountain pose:** Adopt *Tadasana* or 'mountain pose'. Stand tall, feet firmly planted hip width apart, hands loosely by your side. Slightly tuck back your chin and lift your head from the back of your neck. Pretend you are a mountain with your head reaching to the clouds. To others, it just looks like you're standing straight with correct posture. Internally, you are building your confidence and strength by standing tall.

- **Drishti eye gaze:** Drishti is a way of seeing instead of looking. Focus your gaze into the distance. Let your peripheral vision come into focus. Look at nothing in particular and everything at once. This action is imperceptible to others, but internally transforms your attention from yourself, to the space. It helps you 'get outside your own head' and turn your focus to the people who need you in the room.

- **Silence:** Allow moments of silence. A moment of silence can change the mood instantly from one of busyness or frantic energy to one of deep reflection and appreciation. It slows the pace down, and gives everyone a pause to listen to what is going on inside their own heads – so that they can both find and share their voice.

These hacks activate the parasympathetic nervous system, kicking you out of the high-pressure moment and into flow. They activate the neurochemistry of flow and give you the chance to choose your response, instead of your default reaction.

It's no surprise that I learned these techniques in yoga classes. Yoga is just a metaphor for life. Yoga means union of mind, body and spirit. What we learn on the mat is how to flow in and out of challenging poses while maintaining a state of calm by moving with the breath. The asanas (postures) on the mat are practice for the real thing – which is life.

When it finally dawned on me that what I was doing on the mat was learning how to be more centred in life, I realised these techniques can be used anywhere, anytime I feel nervous, anxious or stressed. You don't need to be a yogi to use them, and no-one needs to know you're practicing mindfulness when you're doing it. It's a private communion with yourself during challenging moments, to maintain a steady state and remain available to the experience as it unfolds, without judgement or fear.

State matters more than script. Work on your state, and the rest will follow.

State matters more than script. Work on your state, and the rest will follow.

Part IV summary

- Teams in synergy are calm – they have confidence in the team knowing that together they're better.

- When teams keep calm and find synergy, they've entered an optimal state known as **flow**.

- Our best days are the ones we have flow experiences – a breakthrough, a creative moment, absorption in a task so infinitely engaging that we lose track of time.

- Teams in synergy are in **group flow**. This is the ultimate bonding experience.

- Finding team synergy is a process of turning your focus to the dynamic of the team and enabling each member to take up their roles as simultaneous leaders and followers.

- To find team synergy and create the conditions for group flow, teams need to Get Real, Get Close, and Get Better.

- To **Get Real** involves three conversations – Diagnose, Discuss and Decide.

  - **Diagnose** the group dynamic using measurement tools that capture qualitative or quantitative data on how the group interact.

  - **Discuss** opportunities for improvement by making sense of each team member's experience of being part of the team.

  - **Decide** what needs to change to improve the team dynamic, agree on *the one thing* that will increase the chances of successful behaviour change.

- To **Get Close** we must go deeper. To Get Close teams must Share, Seek and Solve.

  - **Share** more about each other. Find out what makes each team member tick by sharing personal values, strengths and preferences.

- **Seek** feedback. Find and close the gap between one's intention and teammates' perception. Normalising a feedback culture is a proven methodology for improving team performance.
- **Solve** who owns what. Ensure each team member has both *role clarity* and *goal clarity*, so they are enabled to perform.

- To **Get Better** set clear benchmarks for performance. Agree on Purpose, Principles and Prevention.
  - **Purpose** is a powerful tool for aligning teams on a meaningful cause. Define how your team adds value in the service to your organisation's purpose.
  - **Principles** define the explicit norms and expectations for working together. Use your values as a starting point to define principles.
  - **Prevention** is a process for clearing issues. Learning and practicing regular *Issues Clearing* will protect a team against dysfunction and build trust and respect.

- To create safety when working on team dynamics, be a facilitator.
- Facilitators create safety by thinking about how they lead groups through three key stages: pre-workshop, during and after.
  - **Pre-workshop:** Send an email that lets people know what to expect including the agenda, objectives, and what to prepare. Ensure the space you secure is conducive to sharing.
  - **During the workshop:** Facilitation is a specific mode in which you contain the space for people to work through challenges and solve problems. To do this:
    - **Set the scene** by framing the objectives and agenda.
    - **Remove distractions** by asking people to turn off notifications and tune in as a sign of respect.
    - **Role model vulnerability** by sharing a story about why this conversation matters, including your emotions in the story. This sets the scene for others to do the same.

- **Facilitate working sessions** by framing conversations, drawing out the inputs, consolidating the thinking, and agreeing on the outputs or next steps.
- **Close with gratitude** by asking everyone to share their takeaways and what they are grateful to the group for. Ensure you've met the goals and expectations shared at the start.

- **Post-workshop:** The outputs from the workshops are valuable. Capture and distribute these as assets for future conversations.

- Facilitators also create safety by working on themselves to contain their own emotions. State matters more than script. Your state is more important than how you facilitate and even the words you say.

- The paradox of group life is that we want to both be in a group, and still maintain an independent identity. The synergy model solves this problem by encouraging us to be both. To be an independent thinker, and to leverage collective capacity.

- By harnessing the skills to find team synergy, you will future-proof yourself and the communities you serve.

Conclusion on Group Life

The average adult spends a third of their life at work. Team life is an enormous part of work life. While we talk about joining great cultures, what we really want is to join great teams.

There is an inherent paradox to team life. We all have egos – a sense of self that needs to be nurtured as separate from others. Yet we are social creatures – our survival and evolution depends upon our ability to form strong bonds and herd together in social groups. The paradox of group life is that we want to both be in a group, and maintain an identity independent of the group.

The synergy model solves this problem by encouraging us to be both. To be an independent thinker, and to leverage collective capacity. It encourages us to maintain our unique identity and interact dynamically with the identities of others. It encourages us not to fit in, but to belong: Fitting in = conforming to the group. Belonging = group expands to include you.

Find team synergy

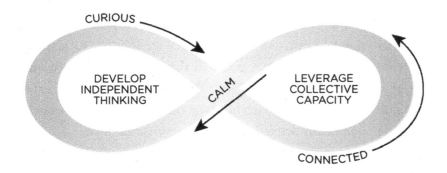

CURIOUS

DEVELOP
INDEPENDENT
THINKING

CALM

LEVERAGE
COLLECTIVE
CAPACITY

CONNECTED

Great teams are curious, connected and calm. Teams who cultivate these qualities find synergy by encouraging independent thinking and working collaboratively to innovate new solutions to challenging problems. Teams in synergy enter group flow more often, actively engaging in challenging tasks and producing extraordinary outcomes in creative ways.

By harnessing the skills to find team synergy, you will future-proof yourself and your organisations. Team players who are skilled at activating collective intelligence, harnessing diverse viewpoints, and containing the anxiety provoked by complex, adaptive challenges, will be the leaders of the future.

> **By harnessing the skills to find team synergy, you will future-proof yourself and your organisations.**

This whole effect is amplified when leadership teams set the tone from the top. How the leadership team interacts sets the example for every other team in the business. The business cannot be fully enabled until organisational leaders stop thinking and working in siloed ways and start thinking systemically.

AI will augment human work, but it will never replace human work. AI frees us of cognitive load and affords us headspace to tackle the tangled web of systemic issues that leaders across all industries face today. These problems will become more complex, not less. The human work of leadership is not something AI can do for us. It is something we must do for ourselves. Correspondingly, these are the skills most at risk through the triple threat of algorithms, attention theft and burnout. We must work better together to activate the enormous pool of human potential that already exists in teams and organisations.

Leaders and leadership teams face unprecedented challenges. Realising potential by activating team synergy is our answer. Do not be afraid to lean in and push your team to be a high-performing team. Your courage, honesty, and genuine intent to build more trusting and resilient teams, will not go to waste. On the contrary, it will build more adaptive, responsive and collaborative communities of practice. If you want to make a lasting difference to the performance and culture of your organisation, community or industry, lead your team to synergy.

Acknowledgements

I can hardly believe that I am in my 10th year running my own practice, and now, at the completion of my second book.

Thank you to those who shared their views and stories to help shape the ideas in this book:

The Honourable David Gonski – it was indeed a career highlight the day my request to interview you was accepted. You took the time out of your busy life to share your thoughts on why boards need to be a team. Thank you for being so generous.

Liz Ritchie – we did our Masters of Organisations Dynamics together and I am so happy our paths have come around again for me to hear your story and to work with your team. Thank you for sharing your experience with me.

Thank you to my editors and publishers:

Erin O'Dwyer from Good Prose Studios – who worked with me as my developmental editor. You encouraged me to find and share more of my own voice and experiences alongside the wisdom of others. The irony is not lost on me! Your helpful comments and journalistic eye ensured this book was both informative and engaging.

Thank you once again to **Michael Hanrahan** and the team at Publish Central. You make publishing an easy and enjoyable experience.

This book I'd like to dedicate to my clients – the people who invite me into their private professional lives, who trust me with their challenges and from whom, through sharing their experiences, I learn so much about our very human need for achievement, fulfillment and growth.

I used to have a beautiful yoga teacher (Januta) who would end every class with the words 'thank you for being my teachers'. At the time I thought it was a strange thing to say. She was *our* teacher and we were *her* students, after all. Until I realised that teaching is itself a form of learning.

Every client is different, every context is unique. While the ideas are the same, I never deliver the same talk or program twice. Learning how to adapt my programs each time I work with a client is how I get better. I have found my calling – to work with leadership teams is my passion and my joy. What an honour it is, to do what I love every day.

I've had so many beautiful clients, but there are a few who stand out as people I'd like to acknowledge as instrumental in shaping my ideas in the four years since I wrote my first book.

Steve Kloss – you have been with me from the beginning of my practice and I am humbled by your continued faith in me. Thank you for your enduring trust, loyalty, commitment to the process and infallible optimism.

Ulrich Irgens – you knew you wanted to make culture a priority, and you were totally committed to putting it on the agenda as a core enabler of rapid growth. You are bold, brave and incredibly talented. It was pure excitement for me to partner with you and your awesome team on the other side of the world. Thank you for the experience and the opportunity.

Marie Brenoe, Michael Frantl and **Katrine Ryberg Johansen** – The Dream Team. Working with you on one of the biggest programs of my professional career was a privilege. You always said YES. Yes to every idea, yes to every suggestion, yes to every change. You are three awesome people who are going on to do awesome things.

Jonas Alexandersson, Casper Henningson and **Ida Thyrring Bredkjaer** – incredible leaders with incredible dreams. Casper's determination, coupled with Jonas' empathy, coupled with Ida's strength is a serious competitive advantage. You will succeed…it is just a matter of time.

David Trewern – just….wow. Your belief, passion, energy, curiosity, capacity and commitment makes you an unstoppable force. You called me when you first moved to Byron because you knew you needed a coach for the adventure you were about to embark upon. Little did I know! Your success has been meteoric (again). You deserve everything coming your way.

Zig Van der Slys – working with you and your organisation was like watching a Phoenix rise from the ashes. You are one of the rare business leaders who is more interested in hearing what your team has to say than being the first to speak. I admire that greatly. Thanks for trusting me to guide you through a difficult moment, and for your continued faith in the process. You are clever like the Fox. Also **Sarah-Jane McQueen** – it's wonderful to work with such a savvy, heart-centred CEO stepping up to the plate.

Julia Davis – you have the most infections energy! Working with you is fun and easy. Your honesty and insight is refreshing. Thanks for letting me steward your future stars.

Dean Haritos – when you're in, you're all in. You're a person of high moral standards and a role model of vales-based leadership. Thank you for your unwavering commitment to the process.

Elliot Solomon – a family man and someone who cares deeply about people. You are the difficult balance of strength and humility. In an industry that fights for every dollar, it's an honour to work with a leadership team who demonstrate synergy each time I see them in action.

Thank you all for being my clients and my teachers.

Finally, and most importantly, thank you to my family who are my reason for being. Clinton, Byron and Lawson. My work takes me away from you for hours, days and weeks, but our times together make it all worth it. Thank you for your love, support and encouragement. Life with you is the greatest adventure.

About Stephanie

Stephanie is obsessed with the collective capacity for all humans to come together in small groups and make a difference. By exploring the bonds that tie and the moments that break, Stephanie inspires leaders to fully turn up, lean in, and leverage collective capacity to achieve outstanding results.

Curious, Connected and Calm is Stephanie's second book. Her first book is *Purpose, Passion and Performance: how systems for leadership, culture and strategy drive the 3Ps of high-performing organisations*. *Purpose, Passion and Performance* was awarded one of Australia's top 3 leadership books in 2021.

As an accredited facilitator for Young Presidents Organization (YPO) and Company Director (GAICD), Stephanie deeply understands the challenges today's leaders face. She works with directors, founders and executive teams to deliver talks and programs that embed high-performance habits and drive transformational change.

Having completed a Masters in Organisation Dynamics, tertiary qualifications in psychology, neuropsychology and positive psychology, as well as five professional accreditations in validated psychometric tools, Stephanie has devoted her life to discovering the dynamics of individuals, teams and organisations at work, and lives to share her insights with her clients.

Following a strong grounding as a management consultant with celebrated consultancy Nous Group, as well as several years as the in-house coach to the executive team at Swisse Wellness who delivered a record private sale of A\$1.6 billion in 2015, Stephanie founded her own practice in Byron Bay, NSW. From there, Stephanie has evolved to deliver thought-provoking content, programs and talks to leadership teams spanning all industries and continents that fundamentally change the way leaders and leadership teams operate.

To connect with Stephanie, reach out to her on LinkedIn, sign up for her regular insights from her website, or reach out directly on any of these channels:

W: stephaniebown.com
E: stephanie@stephaniebown.com
L: linkedin.com/in/stephaniebown1/

References

Part I References

Australian Institute of Company Directors (AICD). (2020, January 1). *Governing organisational culture*. https://www.aicd. com.au/organisational-culture/business-ethics/change/governing-organisational-culture.html

Catmull, E. (2008). How Pixar fosters collective creativity. *Harvard Business Review, 86*(9).

Grant, A. (2018, April). *The best teams have this secret weapon* [Video]. YouTube. https://www.youtube.com/watch?v=hPgY45xsGsU

Lencioni, P. M. (2002). *The five dysfunctions of a team.* Jossey-Bass.

Manpower Group. *2024 Global talent shortage*. Retrieved August 3, 2023. https://go.manpowergroup.com/talent-shortage

Muir, W. M. (1985). Relative efficiency of selection for performance of birds housed in colony cages based on production in single bird cages. *Poultry Science, 64*(12), 2239–2247.

Szumal, J. L. (2000). How to use problem-solving simulations to improve knowledge, skills, and teamwork. In M. Silberman & P. Philips (Eds.), *The 2000 team and organization development sourcebook*. McGraw-Hill.

Wells, L. (1980). The group as a whole: A systemic socio-analytic perspective on intrapersonal and group relations. In C. P. Alderfer & C. L. Cooper (Eds.), *Advances in experiential social processes*, 165–200. John Wiley.

World Economic Forum (WEF). (2023, April 30). *The future of jobs report 2023*. https://www.weforum.org/reports/the-future-of-jobs-report-2023

Part II References

Australian Institute of Company Directors (AICD). (2024, April 9). Australian Governance Summit 2024: At the forefront. https://www.aicd.com.au/good-governance/aicd-australian-governance-summit-2024-at-the-forefront.html

Bain, A. (1998). Social defenses against organizational learning. *Human Relations, 51*(3), 413–429.

Barney, T. (n.d.). *How much time do you lose to distractions?* Workplace trends. Retrieved August 3, 2023. https://workplacetrends.co/how-much-time-do-you-lose-to-distractions/

Church, M. & Cook, P. (2018). *Think: Using pink sheets to capture and expand your ideas.* Thought Leaders Publishing.

De Bono, E. (2009). *Think! Before it's too late.* Random House.

Dweck, C. (2006). *Mindset: The new psychology of success.* Ballantine Books.

Eden, D. & Shani, A. B. (1982). Pygmalion goes to boot camp: Expectancy, leadership, and trainee performance. *Journal of Applied Psychology, 67*(2): 194–199.

Eden, D. & Ravid, G. (1982). Pygmalion versus self-expectancy: Effects of instructor- and self-expectancy on trainee performance. *Organizational Behavior and Human Performance, 30*(3): 351–364.

Felton, O. (2016, March 9). *How to kill good things to make room for truly great ones.* Medium. https://blog.x.company/how-to-kill-good-things-to-make-room-for-truly-great-ones-867fb6ef026

Frankl, V. E. (1959). *Man's search for meaning.* Beacon Press.

Gilbert, E. (2015). *Big magic: Creative living beyond fear.* Penguin Random House.

Grant, A. (2021). *Think again: The power of knowing what you don't know.* Penguin Random House.

Jackson, G. (2023, November 15). *Two charts demonstrating 1,000 years of tech disruption.* Trustnet. https://www.trustnet.com/news/13396044/two-charts-demonstrating-1000-years-of-tech-disruption

Jenner, H. (1990). The pygmalion effect. *Alcoholism Treatment Quarterly, 7*(2): 127–133.

Kashdan, T. B. (2009). *Curious? Discover the missing ingredient to a fulfilling life.* Harper Collins.

Kashdan, T. B. (2013). *Curiosity – the missing ingredient* [Video]. YouTube. https://www.youtube.com/watch?v=_7WMKmGdMIY

Learman, L. A., Avorn, J., Everitt, D. E., & Rosenthal, R. (1990). Pygmalion in the nursing home. The effects of caregiver expectations on patient outcomes. *Journal of the American Geriatrics Society, 38*(7): 797–803.

Merisotis, J. (2021). *Human work in the age of smart machines.* RosettaBooks.

MITRE-Harris Poll. (2023, September 19). *Public trust in AI technology declines amid release of consumer AI tools.* https://www.mitre.org/news-insights/news-release/public-trust-ai-technology-declines-amid-release-consumer-ai-tools

Muthukrishna, M. (2023). *A theory of everyone. The new science of who we are, how we got here, and where we're going.* MIT Press.

PagePersonnel. (n.d.). *The invisible revolution: Talent trends 2023 reports.* Retrieved July 24, 2024. https://www.pagepersonnel.com.au/talent-trends/the-invisible-revolution

Rosenthal, R. & Jacobson, L. (1968). Pygmalion in the classroom. *The Urban Review, 3*(1): 16–20.

Ruppanner, L., Churchill, B., Bissell, D., Ghin, P., Hydelund, C., Ainsworth, S., Blackhman, A., Borland. J., Cheong, M., Evans,

M., Frerman, L., King, T., & Vetere, F. (2023). *2023 State of the future of work*. Work Futures Hallmark Research Initiative, The University of Melbourne. https://findanexpert.unimelb.edu.au/scholarlywork/1758886-2023-state-of-the-future-of-work

Senge, P. (2006). *The fifth discipline: The art and practice of the learning organisation*. Crown.

Sinek, S. (Host). (2024, January 23) A theory of everyone with Dr Michael Muthukrishna (No 111) [Audio podcast episode]. https://simonsinek.com/podcast/episodes/a-theory-of-everyone-with-dr-michael-muthukrishna/

Thorndike, R. L. (1968). Review: Pygmalion in the classroom by Robert Rosenthal and Lenore Jacobson. *American Educational Research Journal, 5*(4), 708–711.

World Economic Forum (WEF). (2023, May 1). *Future of jobs 2023: These are the most in-demand skills now – and beyond*. https://www.weforum.org/agenda/2023/05/future-of-jobs-2023-skills/

Part III References

Australian Human Resources Institute (AHRI). (2023, February 23). *The state of diversity, equity and inclusion in Australian workplaces*. https://www.ahri.com.au/wp-content/uploads/DEI-Report-2023.pdf

Australian Institute of Company Directors (AICD). (2020). *Board size director tool*. https://www.aicd.com.au/content/dam/aicd/pdf/tools-resources/director-tools/board/board-size-director-tool.pdf

Australian Institute of Company Directors (AICD). (2024). *Company Directors Course materials: Governance and the practice of leadership* (p. 42). Course materials available to participants of the AICD company directors course.

Blenko, M. W., Mankins, M. C., & Rogers, P. (2010). *Decide & deliver: 5 steps to breakthrough performance in your organisation*. Harvard Business Press.

Branson, R. (2022, November 1). *Ask Richard: What makes a start-up standout for investment?* [Post]. LinkedIn. https://www.linkedin.com/pulse/ask-richard-what-makes-start-up-stand-out-investment-richard-branson/

Brown, B. (2018). *Dare to lead: Brave work. Tough conversations. Whole hearts.* Random House.

Canva. (2021, September 14). *The importance of diversity at Canva and how we are working on it.* Canva. https://www.canva.com/newsroom/news/The-importance-of-diversity-at-Canva/

Clark, T. R. (2020). *The 4 stages of psychological safety: Defining the path to inclusion and innovation.* Berrett-Koehler.

Clark, T. (2023, January 23). How a CEO can create psychological safety in the room. *Harvard Business Review.* https://hbr.org/2023/01/how-a-ceo-can-create-psychological-safety-in-the-room

Covey, S. R. (1989). *The seven habits of highly effective people: Restoring the character ethic.* Simon and Schuster.

Edmonson, A. C. (2019). *The fearless organization: Creating psychological safety in the workplace for learning, innovation, and growth.* John Wiley & Sons.

Groysberg, B., Abbott, S. L. & Gregg, T. (2020) *Amazon: Cult or culture?* Harvard Business School Case 421-008, November 2020 (revised March 2021).

Guilford. J. P. (1950). Creativity. *American Psychologist, 5*(9), 444–454.

Hunt, V., Layton, D., & Prince, S. (2015, January 1). *Why diversity matters.* McKinsey & Company. https://www.mckinsey.com/capabilities/people-and-organizational-performance/our-insights/why-diversity-matters

Johansson, F. (2017). *The medici effect: What elephants & epidemics can teach us about innovation.* Harvard Business School Press.

Noorgat, B. (2024, February 1). *Mispriced: A deep dive as to why Canva's $26 billion valuation doesn't add up.* [Post]. LinkedIn. https://www.linkedin.com/pulse/mispriced-deep-dive-why-canvas-26-billion-valuation-noorgat-ca-cfa-ppgxf/

Norris, E. (2024). *Diversity and inclusion: Best practices to be a trailblazer.* Marlee: Fingerprint for Success. https://getmarlee.com/blog/diversity-and-inclusion

Rath. T. (2007). *StrengthsFinder 2.0 from Gallup: Discover your CliftonStrengths.* Gallup Press.

Regional Australia Institute. (2023). *Regionalisation ambition 2032. A framework to rebalance the nation. 2023 Year 1 progress report.* https://rebalancethenation.com.au/common/Uploaded%20files/Files/Regionalisation%20Ambition%202032/Regionalisation%20Ambition%20-%20Year%201%20Progress%20Report%20-%20FINAL.pdf

Rittel, H. W. & Webber, M. M. (1973). Dilemmas in a general theory of planning. *Policy Sciences, 4*(2), 155–169.

Sinek, S. (2009, September). *How great leaders inspire action.* [Video]. TED Conferences. https://www.ted.com/talks/simon_sinek_how_great_leaders_inspire_action

Sinek, S. (2019). *The infinite game.* Portfolio.

Sisodia, R., Sheth, J., & Wolfe, D. (2007). *Firms of endearment: How world-class companies profit from passion and purpose.* Wharton School Publishing/Pearson Education.

Sutton, B. (2014, March 4). *Why big teams suck.* [Post]. LinkedIn. https://www.linkedin.com/pulse/20140303152358-15893932-why-big-teams-suck/

Part IV References

Cazaly, L. (2016). *Leader as facilitator: How to inspire, engage and get work done.* Lulu Press.

Church, M., Fink, C., & Coburn, S. (2022). *Speakership: The art of oration, the science of influence.* Phink Enterprises.

Coyle, D. (2019). *The culture code: The secrets of highly successful groups.* Random House.

Csikszentmihalyi, M. (1990). *Flow: The psychology of optimal experience.* HarperCollins.

DiSC profile. (n.d.). *Unlock the potential of your people.* https://www.discprofile.com/

Gallup. (2024). *Learn about the science and validity of CliftonStrengths.* https://www.gallup.com/cliftonstrengths/en/253790/science-of-cliftonstrengths.aspx

Keller, G. (2014). *The one thing: The surprisingly simple truth behind extraordinary results.* John Murray One.

Kotler, S. (2014). *The rise of superman. Decoding the science of ultimate human performance.* Houghton Mifflin Harcourt.

Rath, T. (2007). *StrengthsFinder 2.0. from Gallup: Discover your CliftonStrengths.* Gallup Press.

Sali, R. & Schweidt, B. (2024). *How to build a billion-dollar business: On purpose. For profit. With passion.* John Wiley & Sons.

Sawyer, K. (2007). *Group genius: The creative power of collaboration.* Basic Books.

Sawyer, K. (2015). Group flow and group genius. *NAMTA Journal,* 40(3), 29–52.

The Myers-Briggs Type Indicator (MBTI). (2024). *The MBTI assessment.* https://au.themyersbriggs.com

Walker, C. (2010). Experiencing flow: Is doing it together better than doing it alone? *The Journal of Positive Psychology, 5*(1), 3–11.

Whitmore, J. (2010). *Coaching for performance: The principles and practice of coaching and leadership* (4th ed.). Nicholas Brealey Publishing.

VIA Institute on Character. (2024). *Character strengths profile survey.* Retrieved May 10, 2024. https://www.viacharacter.org/

Addendum: Values Activity

Defining your values is a key step towards living a more mindful life.

Values are what matter most to you. When we are living true to our core values, we feel more fulfilled, content, and experience a greater sense of wellbeing.

IDENTIFY YOUR TOP 5 VALUES

Need inspiration? Think about when you've been at your happiest and most fulfilled – a 'peak' experience in your life. What values were being felt and expressed at that time?

☐ Accountability	☐ Control	☐ Family
☐ Achievement	☐ Courage	☐ Fitness
☐ Adventure	☐ Courtesy	☐ Focus
☐ Altruism	☐ Creativity	☐ Freedom
☐ Ambition	☐ Curiosity	☐ Fun
☐ Assertiveness	☐ Decisiveness	☐ Generosity
☐ Balance	☐ Determination	☐ Gratitude
☐ Belonging	☐ Discovery	☐ Growth
☐ Calmness	☐ Discipline	☐ Happiness
☐ Challenge	☐ Empathy	☐ Hard Work
☐ Cheerfulness	☐ Enjoyment	☐ Health
☐ Commitment	☐ Enthusiasm	☐ Honesty
☐ Community	☐ Excellence	☐ Independence
☐ Compassion	☐ Excitement	☐ Integrity
☐ Contentment	☐ Exploration	☐ Intelligence
☐ Contribution	☐ Faith	☐ Intuition

- ☐ Joy
- ☐ Leadership
- ☐ Legacy
- ☐ Love
- ☐ Loyalty
- ☐ Openness
- ☐ Originality
- ☐ Perfection
- ☐ Positivity
- ☐ Practicality
- ☐ Professionalism
- ☐ Punctuality

- ☐ Quality
- ☐ Reliability
- ☐ Resourcefulness
- ☐ Self-control
- ☐ Selflessness
- ☐ Self-reliance
- ☐ Sensitivity
- ☐ Service
- ☐ Simplicity
- ☐ Speed
- ☐ Spontaneity
- ☐ Strength

- ☐ Structure
- ☐ Success
- ☐ Support
- ☐ Teamwork
- ☐ Thoughtfulness
- ☐ Trustworthiness
- ☐ Understanding
- ☐ Unity
- ☐ Usefulness
- ☐ Vision
- ☐ Vitality
- ☐ Wealth

Name up to five values in priority order, with 1 being the most important.

1. _____

2. _____

3. _____

4. _____

5. _____

Define each value – write a little bit about what our chosen values means to you. Different words mean different things to different people so it's important to define what each value means to YOU in your life.

Value 1
To me means…

_____

_____

_____

_____

_____

Value 2
To me means...

_____

_____

_____

_____

Value 3
To me means...

_____

_____

_____

_____

Value 4
To me means...

_____

_____

_____

_____

Value 5
To me means...

_____

_____

_____

_____

ALSO BY
STEPHANIE BOWN

Leadership drives purpose, culture drives passion, and strategy drives performance. Together, the 3Ps – purpose, passion and performance – equal profit. And profit is the life-giving blood keeping the economy flowing and growing.

"A kaleidoscope of wonderful ideas"
Radek Sali, Former CEO of Swisse Wellness

PURPOSE, PASSION & PERFORMANCE
HOW SYSTEMS FOR LEADERSHIP, CULTURE & STRATEGY
DRIVE THE 3Ps OF HIGH-PERFORMING ORGANISATIONS

STEPHANIE BOWN

How do I maximise the performance and engagement of my people?

How do I create a business where people are motivated to achieve and passionate about what they do?

How do I build my business to be resilient and adaptive in dynamic and volatile markets?

If you are a CEO, founder, director or leader, you can't control what happens in the broader social, environmental or economic context. What you can influence is the way your organisation is set up to respond. What you can do is create the conditions for performance in your business by focusing on the systems that connect, align and inspire your people.

This book is about how you can build a high-performance system which enables your business to adapt to any market condition and weather any storm. It describes and explains how to implement three key systems that enable high performance:

- A leadership system.
- A culture system.
- A strategy system.

If you want to lead a high-performing team, this is your guide to building high-performance systems.